What is Love?

Messages From Mary

On Love and Fulfilment.

Scribed By Maya

Copyright © 2011 Narelle Johnson

All rights reserved.

ISBN-10: 064657079x

ISBN-13: 978-0646570792

This book is dedicated to:

Sananda, Aram, and Arante.

Who patiently persevered with Maya, and lovingly coaxed this

Material out into the Light.

In Appreciation of your Care, Insight & Perseverance.

Contents

Chapter	Title	Page
	Acknowledgements	7
	Preface	9
	Welcome From Mary	11
Chapter 1	Love is Not	15
Chapter 2	Who are You?	33
	Projection Awareness	39
Chapter 3	Projection	51
Chapter 4	Stopping Projection	63
	Tuning In Exercise	81
Chapter 5	Denial Breakthrough	85
	Inner Pond Reflection	105
Chapter 6	Unravelling Love	109
	Unlovableness Questionnaire	126
Chapter 7	Do I look Fat in this?	
	Uncovering Unworthiness	137

	Unworthiness Tour	143
	Opening Up Hearing	153
Chapter 8	**Love Revolution – Receptivity**	**165**
	Childhood Reverie	185
Chapter 9	**Surrender**	**191**
Chapter 10	**Allowing Earth to Disintegrate**	**211**
Chapter 11	**Opening Up The Inner Oasis**	**233**
Chapter 12	**Incorporating Love into Everyday**	**245**

Maya

Acknowledgements

This book could not have been conceived, scribed or brought to fruition without the thankless devotion of one woman Pam Wikstrom, who tirelessly ensured the validity of the information and the energy coming through onto the page. It is only as a direct result of the tremendous energy that she herself makes available to the earth that this small snippet could be brought out into the light.

It is with deep gratitude and thankfulness that I have been privileged enough to be part of this process, and have been able to work alongside such a wonderful, insightful, and gracious person in Pam Wikstrom to bring this information forward. I have been eternally altered, transformed and lifted up by this work, through my interactions with Pam, and as a direct result of learning to recognise and work with these energies.

With heartfelt thanks and inestimable gratefulness

Maya.

Preface

Hello Dear Reader,

My name is Maya, and I am the vessel through which the following information has come forward. I have been channelling for the best part of the last 15 years, and this work has revealed to me how much exists outside our current scope of awareness.

I feel blessed to have been a part of this process and to have had a teacher who could show me what is possible. Although unconventional in method the information contained herein is of great benefit and has helped me enormously – I am indebted to Mary for her gracious patience with me and my moods, and her unfailing faith and flexibility made obvious throughout this process.

In this day and age where we all seem to be chasing love, attention and care her words offer insight into the ways in which our attempts to gain love are secretly pulling us away from who we are. As we will see, it is only by being acutely aware of who we are can we ever hope to sustain a real and permanent sense of being loved.

 I urge you to take Mary's hand, to trust in her, more so than any written word or material, and you will see just how magical and wonderful her energy, her being, her assistance can be...

Cheers Maya xx

Mother Mary – Welcome

Welcome I am Mother Mary – I come forward today to bid you all welcome to this moment in time where I can share my essence and being with you.

I come forward to let you know that you are not alone, and that you do have protectors, guides and beings who watch over and care for you. I see and feel the loneliness that most of you suffer with, I see the pain and anguish at being left, being abandoned, seemingly not good enough for your partner or spouse, your children or parents, friends or colleagues. I know all too well the desperation that most of you feel at times, and I know how futile the attempts you are making at connection and comfort are.

Everyone in your life will and must let you down at some point. Not out of spite, or deliberate callousness, but purely because they must follow their own path and way just as you must follow yours, this must always come first. Suffocating each other under the blanket that you call love and I deem control is no way to force people into loving you being with you, respecting or listening to you. I know the pain of the past leaves you feeling empty and vulnerable, and so you have become more demanding and expectant of those who you are with now, but I assure you, no one else can give you love and acceptance if you cannot offer it to yourself.

I come forward today to light a path of love, a revolution that no longer allows control to be such an integral part of the way you live your lives. I come to offer you freedom from the love that now enslaves you and forces you into obligation and patterns of living which are destructive and a general waste of time for you. When time is always ticking you need to treat your time like a precious resource, like water, not just when at work, when at home too.

Surely all of you can see the difference between your theory of love, and the love that you live with on a daily basis. The love you esteem in your mind is grand and hallowed, effective and real. Yet the love you live with on a daily basis is invisible, indecipherable, lack lustre, demanding and hypocritical. You all love so sweetly in one moment and then the next you are yelling and screaming at each other, to honour this love you must hold your breath, swallow your pride time and time again, if you are to honour its notions and elements.

There is no victory for all with this love, you either win or lose, you do something to please someone, they appear to have won, you have lost, they are the victors of love and you are the loser. There is no even spread with this love, there is no simple oneness or connectedness, it is either them or thou, no room for second place getters. Thus, you will all undoubtedly feel like losers in love, as you will simply have to give way to other people who are more adept at winning love, obtaining love. Whether it is the attention seeker at work who dominates the boss's affections or whether it is your spouse or partner who expect so much of you, either way you will lose. This losing is the subtle cost of the love you have bought into. You pays its price, you become accustomed to losing, as you will make small wins on other days.

Yet, you will not allow yourself to see through it in its entirety as you need to feel loved, you need others to love you and be with you, so that you are not doomed to a life of loneliness. This is after all your greatest fear. So you do the dishes, you put up with your loved ones bad moods, you listen to them preach to you about what you should be doing for them if you really loved them, all the while feeling cheated and betrayed, but hiding it for fear of what conflict might bring.

This is why your divorce rate is so high, eventually someone cannot cope with it anymore, or finds someone that will bow down to them more efficiently. Your ideal of what love is is distorted and corrupt, and the churches your religions have done little indeed to

What is Love? Messages from Mary on Love and Fulfilment

inspire a vision of lasting happiness. You are basically left alone to sort it out for yourself, and in the weight of combined assets, and children are you literally tied to a life of wondering what if?

Now is a time to celebrate, rejoice and cheer, for I have come specifically to speak on love and help you re define it so that you can create a love that is not controlling or suffocating, but free and effervescent, light and fun. Fear not, I have not come to scorn or belittle you and the underhand methods you have used in your love getting to date. I am here to show you a new way, the real way to find a permanent sense of love and ability to be truly loving towards others.

Take heart and know we hear your pleas for help, and this is why we come, to help those of you who will listen, to find a way out from the confusion and dreariness that your mind alone has enslaved you within.

You have much to look forward to

Blessings

Mother Mary

Maya

Chapter One – Love is Not

Greetings my beloved Ones once again,

I come forward today to share with you some ideas about love, so that you can clear out your misperceptions, and begin from scratch to create a different kind of love.

Today in your modern society, with so many boxes and screens on the planet, it appears that in truth you are creating a new kind of love with the screen. It seems as though the screen is the object of all your affection and care, and this may be why you are having even more trouble relating to and listening to your partners. But, firstly let me explain that there are many forms of love, although people tend to lob them all under one heading, love has many different variations and species. Just like a rose or a bird. There is obviously the love a parent feels for their child, the love a child feels for their parent, and this will change as the child ages, and there is the love between siblings, between cousins, aunts and nieces, uncles and nephews, grandparents and grandchildren, neighbours, best friends, brother, sisters, mother and daughter, mother and son, father and daughter, father and son. Then of course there is the phenomenon of falling in love with someone special whether that person is a girl you see on the train, who gets off at the next station and you never see her again, and then there is the love of lovers who are hiding their affection, then of course there is the long term love of a married couple who know each other so well they can almost predict with a high certainty what their spouse will do in any situation, say in any situation, think in any situation.

The dynamic of love then has as many twists and turns as the roads of even your most mountainous regions. Not only this your love appears to grow, change and alter depending on what stage of love you are at, your age, disposition, goals, desires, obligations at any one time in your life affect its availability, potency, and demonstration. So the love you believe in, is like a chameleon, it changes shape and colour depending on what type of love it is, who it is with, and what country you are in, and what phase you are in. There is no wonder then, that you all can become confused and distraught about love, as there is really no clear definition, or device to help you ascertain exactly what phase of love you are in, what the ramifications of this stage are, or even what love is meant to look like at any given stage. Thus are you left to sort it out day by day within your own head, or with your spouse. Thus, the need for marriage counselling has become almost a necessity to help mediate and centre your relationships back on what is important and to not necessarily sweat the little stuff.

But even your counselling has limited success, even this is not infallible or a certain guarantee that all will be well. This is because your multi-coloured ideal of love is not love, never has been love and never will be love. But, this is what you have been taught, you have not had any real role models to teach you differently, and so the love you have grown up with warts and all is the foundation for the love or lack of love that you experience now. It is not really your fault that your love is a failure, but if not you who can I hold accountable? Your society as a whole? Your ancestors? Your priests and reverends? Your parents? No matter who I call forth for judgement, still they will have another to blame, as none of you wish to accept that you alone have accepted this love as necessary and true. You have agreed to this ideal of love, no matter how wretched, unkempt, or scavenous it is. You have used it to get what it is you think you need, and you have allowed others to use it to get them what they think they need. Like using a counterfeit note, you still hand it over even if you realise it is not the real thing, for if the person in the store doesn't realise why should you be the one to give up its value, and besides you can always play dumb if it is just one note.

What is Love? Messages from Mary on Love and Fulfilment

This is what you have done and are still doing to this date. You have turned love into a currency, and you have given money the power and ability to buy you love, and sell it also. The two have become so intermixed and confused that the new generation of children are growing up with no clear definition between the two and parents are paying a high price as a result.

But, still you accept this intermixing, like inbreeding, you are so close to the situation that you cannot see what is wrong with it, it just appears normal to you. Only when an alien species land on your planet and query and demand answers for this type of love will you become red faced and unable to explain exactly how your version of love has become so corrupt.

Even as I tell you this you are doubtful. I will have to convince you further for you to see exactly how distorted your love is, as you are just so accustomed to this love of yours that right now you are a bit perplexed and unsure of what exactly I am talking about. Your love has been polluted to such an extent that like a brilliantly shining crystal clear bay with pale aqua waters, has been turned into sludge and grime the likes of which only an oil spill could create. Your society, your parents, your loved ones, your teachers, and priests, your politicians and clergy have all enforced this idea that love comes from others, and that if you were the only person on the planet then love could not exist.

In other words all of you have bought into the idea that love can only come through someone else, even if that other person is God, Jesus, Mohammed, Buddha, or any of your saints or deities. In other words to be alone, leaves you bereft of love, and this is why being alone is one of the most horrid curses on your planet. This is why computers, and the net, and phones and video cam have become so imperative as you need to have others with you, even if that just means through a screen. This is becoming your new version of love. If you continue in this vain, computers will become your major source of love, and marriage will slowly ebb away from you, intimacy will slowly ebb away from you, authenticity will slowly float out to sea. You have all become so superficial, so easily entertained and amused, that the screens are slowly dominating your affections, distraction, and debate. You are thinking on line, you are conversing on line, you are celebrating on line, you are fighting on line, you are laughing on line, you are creating a real relationship with what you perceive is at the other end of the screen, but unfortunately the screen is not real, and even the people who you meet, and the things that they say are not real, are not true, are not exactly what they appear. This is because they can hide behind the screen, they can keep their secrets, and you will not know, they can dress up anyway they like and you will never know.

Yet, no one seems to question this new allegiance to the screen, it just falls under the category of technology the way of the future. There is no question now, there is no debate, your screens are your future, whether you like it or not, this is the choice you have made. So, rightly so, these new friends will become your closest confidants and allies. You will end up loving them and hating them, just as you now do your families. You will end up using them as more than a tool, a device to gain information from, or contact people, these screens will become almost a part of who you are. So any definition of what your love will be like on Earth 20 – 50 years from now will need to include a clause or consideration of the screens.

Thus even your definition of love is evolving and will continue to evolve as you move throughout this century. You may see nothing wrong with this currently, but sure enough when its effect falls at your feet you will see how these definitions and considerations can harm and effect. But, I am not here to speculate about your future, I am not here to coax you into another form of societal organisation. I am here to share with you my perceptions on love, and what love is not. Love certainly isn't anything that you can obtain from or through a computer, if you are in doubt try hugging a screen and you will gather exactly what I am speaking about.

Yet, you will persist, the computer appears to offer everything you need, information, conversation, good humour, intelligence, they can be tall dark and handsome or stocky bald and weird looking but you will never really know. Of course the computer has its advantages you can all daydream that you are talking to all these really hot people, like you do on the computer games, who are not so hot, not so becoming in real life. It really doesn't matter to you in the end does it? As long as you are getting the attention you need to feel loved and popular, and part of the team this is all you really need.

The love that you have on Earth then is not that inspiring, it is all about you, and how to get you what you want. It doesn't really have anything to do with patience, and understanding and forgiveness, it is more about you feeling part of the group. This has been your main misconception about love. Even without your full awareness your ideal of love is self centred, it is based around your needs. Just like everything else in your life, love is based around you. Everything you read and see on TV, everything you witness down at the shopping plaza, everything you hear about is all interpreted by you and your inner needs, desires and wants. It cannot be any other way. It is not your fault that love has become little more than your own little game of getting you what you want, this is what everyone else is doing too, this is what society teaches you, and this is the way you interpret it within because of the pain, guilt and shame that you hold there. If you did not hold this guilt, shame and pain then it would be easier to interpret love or loving in a different light. You may even be able to grasp a higher type of loving. But, while you are bound by your childhood memories of the lack of love you received are you then destined to interpret love in this manner.

Even if getting what you want means you have to please someone around you, do everything for them, make them a cuppa, do the dishes, give them your money, give them all your time and energy, even if you are doing all this and it appears to be selfless and loving, you are in truth doing this for yourself as you have deemed the person you are doing all this for as the source of your love, and so to receive their love you must please them. On the surface many things seem different, you could easily think that you are being loving, when you volunteer to do the dishes to save conflict, but in truth you are just avoiding conflict or attempting to please the other so that they can be happy and you can remain in their good books. No one, no one likes being outside the loop.

No matter how much you might despise your spouse, or hate some of the things they do, underneath you are seeking their attention and favour just like your children seek yours.

This is what love has become it has become like money, it is currency, that can be bought and sold. It is used to control others to get what you want no matter how humble or giving it may appear on the outside. All of you have fallen into this pit, this pit of thinking love is something you must buy from others. This is what has let your whole species down, this is what has negated your definition of love, so that it like your waterways has become polluted and rotten. Now is the time to see that love has nothing to do with other people and everything to do with you and how you feel inside your being and yourself.

Love is not something you can buy, if you could have bought it all your princes and princesses, your millionaires and billionaires would be on cloud nine, but are they, no, they are more uneasy about love than you. They are more confused and estranged from love than the hobo who lives by the river, they have seen how money and power corrupt and destroy life, love and family. Love is separate and above that of your definitions. Love is a state of being that you reach when you feel connected to where you are, who you are with, and content with all and everything. No one is excluded from this love, they cannot be, as this love is a deep connection to all and everything, the birds in the sky, the water in the river, the rocks in the Earth, the trees by the road, all are equal. Love cannot differentiate, as it comes from within you and your perception, there is no greater love for a soul mate, a love of your life, this is currency, this is need, love is complete and unaffected by the form or face that it sees.

Jesus was attempting to show you this while he was on Earth, this was his message. Not the fact that he died on the cross to save you, to riddle you with guilt and shame and adoration only for him. Jesus wanted you to see the way in which he loved while on Earth, he wanted you to feel the quality of his love, the broadness, and scope. He came to light a new way of interacting on Earth, to light a way for renewed love which was unbiased, and unpolluted by judgement and class, race, or sex. Still today even your greatest clergy have trouble with this. That is because they sought to create a religion, a rule, to control and dominate others rather than learn the lesson themselves, for greater awareness, happiness and peace within them.

When you cannot feel the essence of what Jesus was portraying, when you cannot sense the love in his being, when you have no pathway to feel or know this higher love of understanding, gratitude, and inclusiveness, then seemingly you have no recourse but to interpret his actions in another manner which seeks to force people into doing the right thing, rather than coaxing them through the pure feeling, joy, and love they experience as they spend time with him, his words, his essence. Making rules about love, commandments, etc really undoes even the best of intentions, as when you are forced to do something because this is what is expected, it becomes a burden, you are doing it then to please others, and to stay in peoples good books rather than anything else, this then is perhaps what taught all of you that love is a type of currency?

Jesus gave you all a new commandment to replace all the others, love your brothers as I have loved you. Yet, somehow this has been lost in translation, the commandments still stand they are still the backbone of all of your rules, laws, and governments, and societal ways and institutions. You all must meet these standards unless become a person who is less than perfect, who is sub human, grotesque, without good morals, an oath, simple, uneducated or self serving. Yet, the more you esteem these morals the more your society falls in the opposite direction. Still thwarted with hate killings, growing rage between nations on a daily basis, growing hatred between races who live in the same town, growing mistrust, growing violence, alcoholism and other forms of addiction, all because you have misinterpreted Jesus's original meaning and purpose.

If love excludes, you have judged, how can it then be considered love? Love is the cure to judgement and blame, hatred and separation. Love promotes connectedness, acceptance and trust. Excluding people from the list of people you love is the opposite of love, it is judgement, blame and unacceptance. You have therefore accepted the idea that love is a currency, that it can be bought and sold to the highest bidder, the person who appears to do the most to be worthy of your love, and thus you exclude those who do not do what they have to do to earn your love. This is why people get left out of wills, this is why people divorce, this is why children dobb each other in, this is why people commit suicide, this is why people have affairs. The time has come to see that it is not the people in your life who have let you down, it is the definition of love that you have put your trust and faith in.

Love is not a complicated term, it cannot be you all throw it around so loosely, you make far more out of it than what it actually is. You each define its meaning by your own standards and desires. And these standards and desires fluctuate according to the type of day you are having and the mood you are in. The love you give others is different to the love they must give you. The definitions for all your terms and and ideas change, according to what you want to see and what you don't want to see. If you don't want to see your life as miserable and lonely you develop a term of love that somehow covers over the void you feel within. The fact that you live alone and do not have that someone special. You term love to be about good friendship, the love between you and your children, the political love of charity, all become more esteemed and emphasised. Yet, for someone who is newly in love, the person of their affections is central to what love is, your definition becomes centred on the feelings evoked between two lovers, and the heights that these two people reach within this cocoon of love.

Love can be colored and defined in many different ways and with many different terms, this is because there is no single definition that has been accepted, all of you see it slightly differently and this leaves even greater room for interpretation and misinterpretation. When you are angry you do not think about being loving, when you are sad you do not think about being loving, normally sadness comes from losing a supposed source of love. Love is then something intangible which can be wielded like a sword to win an argument, or to get someone to do what you want, what they want, or it can be forgotten about completely if the situation requires this.

There is then lofty gaps within your definitions of love, and because love is what all of you claim to seek, it then requires some diligence or effort on your part to ensure that what you are looking for actually exists. If I were you, I would make very certain that what I thought I longed for actually did exist, and could give me the satisfaction that I hoped it would.

You however, have not sought to question love too thoroughly, you have merely accepted the idea of not being alone as being loved. If there are people living with you, who are willing to put up with you then you must be loved. If you have people to call on in your time of need then you must be loved. If you have a ring on your finger, if you have children, then your requirements for love are seemingly automatically met. This is why you all seek to find love, get married and have a family. This has created your status quo, this has isolated and left out those people who like being alone, who enjoy being alone and puts undue pressure on them to conform, to mate, to reproduce. Even those couples who initially decide they do not want children, normally end up conforming and doing so by either accident, or design as to be outside the loop can be felt quite blatantly at times. When you sense the void within you, then it is natural to think that perhaps children will fill that void, love will fill that void, a mate will fill that void.

How mistaken this perception is, trying to coat over this void only creates undue aggravation and dissent. Lovers begin to resent each other silently, underneath their breath, for nothing can fill that void, and stuffing another person into it, certainly only makes things worse. Like pouring sulphur onto a volcano do these ideas backfire and only add to the stress of everyday living, making people gradually more sceptical of love, bitter and more likely to shut down from love, living, life, and others.

This is what has happened to your divorcee's, they have become fussier about who their next partner will be and slower to enter a committed relationship, seeking out other addictions instead, to cover over their disappointment about love and life, and their place within it. Normally divorced singles either re enter relationship quickly or they take a long time, the longer they take the more the chances heighten that they will not meet another person who does not scare them excessively. Normally a string of bad relationships follow as a result of their anger over the past, their inability to forgive, to let go of the past, to be loving, to allow and trust life. Thus slowly inch by inch your modern world is filling with isolated people whose only solace is companionship online, as this makes them feel safer, more in control, less likely to get hurt.

It is interesting to note though how people select a partner. Most of you would term it chemistry, there is a drawing, an attraction. Normally they say opposites attract, and to some degree this is the case. Normally however the human species continue to recreate the past, so when selecting a mate, you will select what is familiar from your past. It is the better the devil you know syndrome again. Different spouses may reflect different qualities of people from your past, your first husband might reflect the abusive drunken father that you had, and your second husband may reflect either that same feeling that you felt with your drunken father but in another way, he may not betray you through alcoholism, he may be a workaholic instead, but still betrays you time and time again as work becomes the aim and you are left to one side. Or, your second husband may reflect the gentler qualities of an uncle that you were deeply fond of.

Normally women who have been controlled in their first marriages tend to want to control the other in their second marriage as this is what makes them feel safe. Men too will choose according to whether they want to dominate or please. Either way, the past is influencing all of your decisions and attractions. When you become aware of this, when you can see what mates you have been drawn to in the past and what mates you are drawn to now, there will be obvious differences and also obvious similarities. In the end you are merely selecting obvious qualities that meet your approval, yet underneath there will always be qualities that you detest. Even if a woman remarries a gentle man after a aggressive first marriage, she will secretly resent the impishness of this man, as something within her wants the fire, the passion, the confrontation offered by a macho male, and she will push her new gentle spouse beyond the limits of human endurance in a bid to get some spark, some fire ignited within this new male who is weak and cowardly and introspective.

Men too push the women who attempt to please and adore them, they push them away, and they seek the independence that is free from clinginess, from need, from affection. They have no respect for these women who are not forthright and up front. Thus the inevitable drama and crisis plays out, between the hot headed male angrily demanding things of the woman, and the woman recoiling into her shell in a bid to protect herself. The more she recoils the more he will pursue her, the more she clings and needs and wants the more he will rebut and walk away and not care.

This is why they say opposites attract, as one seems to be pursuing the other fleeing. There are rare relationships where both come together mutually with an evenness and calm. Only friendships which turn into intimate relationships manifest in this way. Friendship really should be more admonished, and people should consider dating their friends more on earth, as overall you would all end up much more content.

Yet you all suffer with the Adam and Eve syndrome you all want what you can't have, you all fall for those who have not fallen for you. So you must either wait, convince, or give up in despair as there are no other options. This is why love is associated with pain on your earth, love has been secretly labelled over symptoms such as ugliness. Unbeknown to all of you you all suffer with the idea that you are not good enough, are ugly, etc you believe wholeheartedly that you are not worthy of love, so any interpretation of love that you have must lay across this divide. Thus your search for love uncovers greater feelings of not being lovable as you seek those who do not seek you, you look for people who do not exist, you look for an absolute, someone who is your definition of perfection, or what seems to be. When you find the object of this perfection normally they do not notice you, they are preoccupied looking for their perception of perfection and normally it does not include people like you. Thus, people find rejection and unhappy unions more so than perfection or a happy union.

This flares up the feelings of unworthiness that all of you suffer with, even those who think they have met perfection soon discover that there is an underside to perfection and that causes them just as much grief as those who experience unrequited love. So unworthiness must be included in your definition of love as this is what you have to deal with while in relationship, these are the feelings and thoughts that are constantly being prodded. Yet, you still think it is your spouse or loved on who is the cause of your pain and anguish, they are uncaring, hostile, cold, selfish, but in truth it is your own feelings of unworthiness which are the culprits of your state of mind.

But, no this is not so, you have done nothing wrong and yet your spouse is betraying you, belittling you, yelling at you, you are of course the victim it cannot be any other way. Your thoughts have little if anything to do with the running of things, your thoughts of shame, guilt and vexation are neutral. They cannot impact or influence the situation, they have absolutely nothing to do with your spouse's bad mood. You are innocent, everyone else is guilty, is wrong, is insane and cruel. These thoughts of blame, of judgement in your eyes have nothing to do with what happens to you. But, from my perspective these thoughts are so strong and imbedded within you that you could not see anything else but rejection and punishment, as this is all you will allow into your life. You do not believe you are worthy of more, you will not allow, or the thoughts repressed within you will not allow you to see anything else but what they dictate. These thoughts are control freaks, they want to imprison you within them, and no one, absolutely no one has the right or the know how to question or second guess them.

Everyday someone will attempt to be nice and loving and generous to you, if not in deed in thought or feeling, someone you know and love but who lives far away will be thinking of you, feeling for you. Everyday something will go right in your life, a stranger will smile at you, the sun will come out to warm you up on those chilly wintery mornings, the flowers in your garden will come out to cheer you up, the children near you will play and laugh, but all this goes unnoticed by you, this and much much more. For the thoughts of not being good enough, of being a failure, of being stupid, torment you, dominate you, and enclose you within a prison of having to prove yourself, so that you can prove these meaningless thoughts wrong or futile.

I have come to tell you these thoughts are already meaningless. You need do nothing, they are like leaves in the wind, let them go and they will vanish never to litter your manicured lawn again. But you cling to them and grab at them like they are $100 notes the more you have the better off you are. You want them in your mind, as the pain they induce if you were to look at them is unbearable, so instead you pretend they do not exist that you are not the creator of your world, and that everything that happens to you is random and unforeseeable, chaotic and unjust.

I can see how this viewpoint would make it easier for you, to some extent, you do not have to take responsibility for anything. You can get by and survive life, relatively well, you can pretend your thoughts are not influencing what happens in your life, you can pretend that you are not the reason bad things come into play, so then you cannot get blamed for anything, you can pretend that it is God, or the Universe, the Earth, or the Governments which are out to get you, are at fault, or are the cause of much of your heartache and persecution, but in reality this is just not so. Somewhere inside you you can feel, sense and know that this cannot be the way such a magnificent eco system works. Of what good would it be to live in such a diversely beautiful planet, with freedom to potentially do anything you want, and yet be a slave to the whim of some old hairy, long bearded man on a throne in Heaven, who only wants you to deny this potential so that you can praise and adore him?

What is the point to a life where your father in Heaven demands your obedience and full attention, when fulfilling this requires denial of your right to explore, create and choose amongst this diversity and apprehends your free will, making you a slave to the dogma of servitude. Is God so dumb so naive that he cannot see your resistance and hesitation to give up these offerings for him? Is he so arrogant that he wants his own children to forsake these delectable fruits even though he knows they will still secretly yearn for these fruits, and in the end despise and resent him for having to deny their own needs and intuitions for the throne? Does your God as omniscient as he is really demand this of you, so that you must endure your whole life living with shame and guilt and a huge sense of unworthiness just because you are born of original sin or think about another man's wife?

Who is this God you have created out of the scripture who is so demanding, cold, unrelenting and unforgiving that you must constantly seek his affection and forgiveness. My question is why? Why would God if he exists at all want this from you? Your God seems to enjoy judgement and persecution, he enjoys making you pay, he enjoys making you squirm. How are you meant to live a positive, happy carefree life, when you have this demanding old goat watching your every move and thought? No wonder you are all so ashamed. You have been indoctrinated into a false belief that your God cares about your small thoughts, and selfish pursuits. Why would he care? He encompasses all and everything, he created this platform for you to enjoy, dance and celebrate his and your existence. Why would he then care, or be concerned that you are doing what you are meant to be doing, what he created this platform for, to enjoy and extend yourselves, to dance, and express the divine joy that is all of ours inherent birthright?

Don't you think God enjoys your enjoyment? Like watching small children play in the back yard, don't you think God enjoys watching you explore and use the world he has created for you? If he hasn't created it for you, of what purpose is it? So that he can demand your eternal love and affection when you are already a part of him? Can you see how absurd this notion is? Can you see how ineffective and imbalanced your religious beliefs are? They do not make any sense. If they are to make sense God is an ogre, God is unforgiving, his intelligence and care limited and your decision to like or hate him much more influential than it should be to an omniscient God. Even children can see the contradiction and lunacy of religion, but you just keep on theorising, you keep on debating amongst yourselves, and you place strong emphasis on words in the bible that you resonate to, just to make your religion true, real or somehow necessary.

I am Mary, I come not to scorn or belittle you. I come not to make fun, of a religion which all of you are very passionate about. For those of you who are not religious still carry the conditioned seeds of religion, you still honour the commandments, you still believe in right and wrong, good and bad, heaven and hell. I have come to set you free, I have come to let you know that a new way of interpreting what you have learnt is available to you, and this new way will be necessary if you are to trespass through this epoch of time securely. Without harming your homes, friends or loved ones too dramatically.

Now is the time to be aware of the games your mind is playing on you, and now is the time to start questioning your beliefs and perceptions, for my dear friends, it is these which are letting you down, running you ragged, and forcing you all into a pattern and style of life, which is becoming more and more alien and unnatural to you. If you do not take stock of where you as a species are headed you will lose contact with what is real and what is not, and you will be forever lost in a land of plastic waste, inconsiderate superficial machines and people who like lost souls ravage you for everything worthwhile that you have.

What is Love? Messages from Mary on Love and Fulfilment

Maya

Chapter Two – Who are You?

Oftentimes one is led to believe that what you are is what you do or what you become. People think that their job defines who they are, their children define them, being a mother, a father, is part of their purpose in this life. Being as good as one possibly can at parenting, at the work they do, is given high esteem and credence. Attaining all the virtues of love, acceptance, forgiveness, patience, and kindness are the epitome of what you are or will become. This is in your view is the highest acclaim of your life, this is who you are when you attain it. This makes you a saint, a good person, this makes you worthy of love, and this makes your life and living worthwhile.

Many believe that it is not what happens in your life which defines you, it is how many people love you and the quality of that love. So accumulating people around you who love you unconditionally is one of your main aims and goals as you age and become a little smarter. This acceptance from others is like a drug you crave it like addicts white powder, you chase it like addicts chase department store sales, you need it like workaholics need to keep their minds active with work so they do not have to think about what is really happening in their lives.

But being loved by others, nurturing politeness and good will within you, is not who you are, they at best can only be part of who you are or a reflection of who you are. Who you are pertains to the source of your origin, are you of God, if so who is God, what is it? Sometimes God is just a label people use to generalise without really knowing what this represents. If you do not stem from some higher magnetic, omniscient force then where do you come from, what has given rise to your existence? Blood and bones alone do not have the momentum to create, to reproduce, to mutate, to grow, evolve and change according to the environment. For this some force is needed, some momentum, some interweaving of life, chemistry, physics and biology. To sustain life, many many variables must come into play at certain times just to enable life to continue.

Whatever this force is, and whatever you believe it to be, whether it is a type of God, whether it is God, whether it is just micro biology, or fusion of matter, gravity, something must have given rise to who and what you are. Whatever this is, must be who you are, as it is the foundation on which everything that you believe you are has sprung. Your personality traits, your ambitions, beliefs, your goals, the things that happen within your life, are not you. Even the thoughts you think are not you as they change and pass so quickly. What you are must be permanent, as opposed to temporary for the substance that has made you, and is you, has also composed and created everything else that you see feel and hear.

It cannot be any other way, life continues, it ebbs and flows, but continues. Whatever magic enables the fertilisation of the zygote, the egg, whatever variables come together to enable a planet to breed life, to sustain the life, must be the essence of it. This means that like all metal, you can be reduced to your purest form, and that purest form is life. Like ants or large flocks of birds, many can work or fly in unison, can navigate without seeming communication between them, to achieve some aim. Some instinct, some force is guiding all of them to act in a cohesive and efficient manner. This life force is who you are – you may be your own unique expression of it, but once you are melted down to your purest form this is what and who you are. This means your mind alone is not who you are. Thus the thoughts, beliefs etc in your mind, do not accurately reflect who you are either, as your mind is connected to all others through this life force. The thoughts in your mind could have been picked up through this connection unwittingly on your part from other minds. So you have no way of knowing who you are just by looking at the thoughts in your mind. They are not trustworthy, reliable or permanent.

To know who you are to even have a taste of it, you must go beyond thought, you must go to that part that enable brain dead people to exist, that enables people to exist in a coma for years on end, that enables people frozen in water to come back to life. You must find this secretive, essential part of which you are, for until you know who you are, how can you know what it is you need to exist? Without tasting this magical part of yourself I can argue that you really have nothing to live for, as your actions and thoughts are robot like, they mimic each other, you are a slave to whatever whimsical thought enters your head. You have no choice, no say, no control, you must get jealous if a jealous thought enters your head, you must get angry if an angry thought or pattern of thoughts enters your head, even if you try to suppress them, they are there and the anger will come even if somewhat delayed. You in essence have no freedom, no exuberance, and no vitality while out of contact with this part of you that enables you to function and breathe. Until such a time that you are, you cannot know what real love is, as you do not even know who you are, and if you do not know who you are, you cannot feel or see the benefits of love.

While you are unable to see or gauge what benefits love actually has on your inner essence, you are handicapped in a sense, you cannot even know if the love that all of you value is assisting or hindering your inner essence, maybe the effect is indifferent? To really appreciate love, to know that the love you are offering is real, to know the love you are receiving is real you need to see its effect on your inner essence, the core of life, if it has no impact on this, then love may not be the grand healer that all of you think. For if love has no permanent effect of what real value is it? If it cannot help you to bridge the gap to your inner self, this life force that has given rise to who you think you are, then its value is minimal and possibly even illusory.

Please know that I come forward to assist all of you to see clearly, not undermine or sabotage your effort towards love. I want the love you bend over backwards for to be real and lasting and effective. All too often in your life you have accepted without question other people's vision and interpretation of love, without even contemplating at times this loves value and meaning for you. Of course having people around you who need you and love you makes you feel better, makes it all seem worthwhile, it is cosy and comforting, warms the cockles of your heart so to speak, but will it last? Does it console you when your drug addicted mentally affected son is berating and humiliating you in public? Does love soothe you then? Does knowing he loves you underneath take away the pain of these situations? Does the love and support you receive from other family members really eradicate the pain and the heartache of watching your addicted son destroy everything and everyone in his life that he cares about?

Does love really help to heal you when you feel alone and misunderstood by those who are closest to you? Does chatting with friends really perpetuate greater stamina in dealing with the atrocities of life, or does it merely distract you for a time? In the end life is going to hit you in the face day after day after day and love, peace, happiness cannot protect you or shield you from this. Love cannot stop your boss from demanding increasing work hours, it cannot stop lonely old work colleagues making inappropriate suggestions, it cannot pay your bills, it cannot lower interest rates, or the cost of fuel or groceries. So really of what value is this love? Where is it? Why does it become invisible when you need it most? Why does it demand of you, but offer so little in return?

Why have you failed to look more closely at this love to date? Is it because you are so busy fulfilling its requirements that you do not have time to assess and evaluate its value? Surely you have felt firsthand the bitter disappointment of even the most torrid of loves and affairs when after its climax has been reached it declines and peters out almost into a type of slumber leaving you with nothing but spite and resentment towards your loved one. When in truth it was not your lover who let you down, but the idea that love could be bought and sold, remaining constant and unchanged when everything else in this life has an expiry date. So like age, wine, virgins and success love has an expiry date. What you do after this is an unknowable consequence of the love that you have so ardently put your faith in.

It is time now to look more closely at this allegiance to love, and to more importantly needing love. Needing someone else, needing to fit in, needing approval, needing to be seen as necessary, good, lovable. Why should you look at this perhaps you are asking? To ensure that you are getting value for money I respond. Can you imagine the difference to your life, yourself, your family, if there was no need? If you did not have to please others to stay in their favour, if you did not have to pile obligation upon obligation upon your shoulders to ensure you are taking care of everything and everyone, to ensure you are a good mother, a good father, a good child, a good sibling. Your society appears to be constantly inventing ways for you to prove you love others, apparently this makes love more real, more see able, more satisfying. Not only are there birthdays, Christmas, Easter, and anniversaries to show you care, now there is valentine's day, mother's day, father's day, and perhaps soon children's day. You continue with this pattern with tree day, red nose day, yellow daffodil day, jeans day all these days just so you can be prompted to care, to give money to raise awareness of the plight of others. Never has a society been more accosted with care.

Yet, this charade of care, does nothing to soothe your inner torment, your pain, your fears, your irrational ideas and thoughts, your restlessness. Nothing can cure you, nothing that you have previously tried, and certainly not, needing others, loving others. Only by seeking a more permanent love a more genuine care, a less burdened concern will you be able to ease the disruption within your mind. If the un ease is in your mind, it makes sense that you must search within here to find its cause and solution. Yet still life dangles another carrot in front of you, and you are off chasing another promise of love, another victory, another job, another holiday, all of which will be the thing you need to de stress, to calm this gnawing sensation and restlessness that creeps up on you and fuels your addictions and compulsions.

Love cannot come from others, love cannot heal you no matter how much you may want it, yearn for it, or crave it. The qualities the object of your affection hold may be traits you would like to develop for yourself, but normally, they are reminding you of something or someone whom gave you comfort while young or perhaps even in another time and place. This association with the past has nothing to do with the now, projecting ideals or characteristics onto others which they may or may not possess will do little to assist you in the long run, and will be the reason love withers so quickly.

Everyone is a screen, and you project onto them that which you wish to see. At times you want to see evil at others you want to see good, but as they say beauty is in the eye of the beholder, you are creating and sustaining everything that you see, from your mind projector. Think about this, why should one person contain all the qualities you hate and despise simply because they made an honest remark about your attire, while someone who may have thought the same thought but did not say anything can be held in high esteem. Everything is relative, relative to you, relative to what thoughts you give credence to within your mind. There is no escaping the perceptions of your mind, unless you seek to delve within it, uncover what thoughts are fuelling your emotions and biases and clear them away so that you can be free to enjoy a vast, light, bliss filled mind un contaminated with judgement.

I appreciate that what I am saying is not commonplace, is not readily or easily grasped, but that does not change the value at its core. More and more your psychologists are turning to thought therapy, to mindfulness, to going within. Forgiveness, acceptance, surrender, all these qualities have been spoken of but forgotten time and time again as they like the turnip are unappealing next to the carrot of life, and having, and getting. If you can start to contemplate the idea that you are projecting onto others what you want to see and don't want to see within yourself, you will then be able to move forward with me, and the remaining information that I will share with you. If you cannot accept and contemplate this idea, you will struggle to appreciate and resonate with other ideas that I will bring forward here. Thus it is important that you contemplate the idea of projection, so I will offer an exercise here, for those of you who are game to use and experiment with, so that you can fully understand and grasp that which I am attempting to convey.

Projection Awareness Contemplation

Releasing restriction from your mind is about owning up to your own shortcomings, and self sabotaging behaviours. One of the main ways in which you sabotage yourself is to believe the thoughts in your mind, and carry out their demands. Believing in the faults of your friends and loved ones and enemies does little to free your mind from the mire of life. To heal this you need to see through projection your minds trick to keep you under its belt. Looking at other people's faults is only helpful if you can feel how these faults make you feel.

Projection is your minds focus on others, whether blame or praise, in a bid to divert you away from the awareness of your own beliefs and behaviours which are secretly harming and killing you. Today we will begin to look at these and the way in which your mind will distract you.

Begin by closing your eyes, counting backwards from 10 slowly and taking deeper slower breaths with every count. Once you have reached zero feel or imagine yourself falling freely inside yourself for a few moments. Reach forward inside your mind after this for a recent person who has upset you, preferably someone that you do not like that much, it may have even occurred today, or yesterday. Look at the incident, then look at the person who has upset you, look at how angry you are at them, even though you may love them dearly. Look at how you see luminously their selfishness, their aggression, materialism, greed, stubbornness, bull headedness, deceit, cunning, and despotic carelessness. Now remember a time which is recent in which you and this same person appeared to see eye to eye, you got along well, even if you doubt there is such a memory look for even a few moments of cordial polite conversation or discussion. Once you have located this memory look more closely at how you felt during this interaction, even though you may not have trusted them fully, or still doubted their sincerity, look at how you feel about them in this moment. Are all the same qualities you just attributed to them with the last memory still there? Or have some of them faded or totally disappeared? Look honestly at what you see and feel in regards to this same person. Are they as bad tempered? Are they as uncivilised? Are they as stupid or as dumb? Are they likable even in this moment? Although it may not change them or your perception or relationship with them, how do they appear within just this small memory?

Have they become more attractive physically perhaps or at least not as ugly or revolting? Have they become more appealing in any sense? Do you find yourself having greater compassion or understanding for them? Look at this memory within your mind, and see how your mind can change your attitude to these people depending on what situation you are in, and how heard, loved, and appreciated you feel. Look more closely at your feelings in regards to this to finish this exercise. Look at how fleeting and changeable your feelings can be depending on your mood, your perception, your need to see what is wrong with others, as opposed to your need to see what is good with them.

Now remember an incident in which someone whom you love dearly and care for significantly, abused, or yelled or scorned or judged you, yet you remained loving and concerned, and un perturbed by their outburst. Look at your feelings, look at how you brush aside their behaviour as a one of, see how you excused them, they are tired, drunk, overworked, stressed etc.

Look at how you maintain your love for them regardless of what they do? Look at how they behave in comparison to the initial person who easily can upset you, with the slightest word or utterance? Who is looking better when you compare the two in an honest light? Does the behaviour of the person whom you do not like that much outweigh the behaviour of the person who you love? Or are you biasedly storing hate towards one, so that you can maintain your love for the other?

Look at the difference in the way you treat these two people. Can you see how your feelings about them have nothing to do with them and who they are, and even what they do, but more to do with your feelings, and your desire to either reinforce a relationship or severe one.

This is projection, this has nothing to do with reality, this is about you and your desire to escape the truth, so that you can maintain what you know and feel comfortable with. If you can see this, you will have made much headway today, please work as solidly as you can with this exercise until you can see clearly what I am attempting to convey.

Who are You Continued.

Following on from the previous section we now need to take a closer look at the parts that actually make up who you are. If you do not know what forces combine to make you what you are, you will never truly know if the love you value is real or false. If you do not know what makes you tick anonymous parts of yourself may influence too easily yourself perception, your beliefs about love, and distort what you see in regards to this love in your world. Thus it becomes imperative to look closer at the ways in which you ignore certain people's behaviour so that you can protect your love, and the ways in which you can severe the possibility for love with people whom you judge cannot offer you it.

Basically your mind is categorising and judging moment to moment. The mind does this as it needs fuel, and judgement is like oil. You soon learn as a child to value more those close to you those who are more connected to your sense of love and worth. Adults who rear you are given precedence over anyone else while you are very little. Then gradually as you age, you will broaden this circle of people you deem lovable, and capable of providing you with a steady stream of love. Those people who are not deemed lovable by you, or with whom you do not care if you do or do not receive love from are relegated to the back of the line, and you use them to manifest hate, vengeance, hostility, competition, anything that is deemed unworthy or dangerous to mix with those who have previously gained your affection.

Throughout life, this categorisation will influence and guide many of your behaviours, your preference for certain kinds of people will sway your decisions about who you mix with, who you are friends with, even what classes you take and those which you don't or skip. Your preferences for a certain type of person will influence your decision about which job to take, and it will influence your employers mind about whether to hire you or not. These preferences are so inbuilt that they occur automatically and you do not even know that you are making them. This is part of your make up, this selection process is part of who you are. This will influence where you perceive you can gain love from and where you perceive you will receive judgement and scorn.

The good friends you made while young will influence new friends you make when older, if someone reminds you of a good friend you had in primary school, the chances then increase that you will form a lasting friendship with them. If someone reminds you of someone whom you had conflict with at primary school or who you did not like, the chances increase that you will not become friendly with them, no matter how keen they may be to be your friend. Throughout your whole life, this preference is operating under the surface. This is what helps form attraction to a certain or potential mate, and what is underlying many of your relationship difficulties and problems.

When you can see how you choose the people in your life, when you can see that you have certain preferences for love, you will also see how this pattern of behaviour also closes you down to love, and living, and is the reason why many spend the later part of their lives alone and unhappy. If you can be aware of this trait within you you can then avoid its pleas to ignore someone, or give them the cold shoulder when in truth they could be underneath the love of your life. Attraction has more to do with this than it does looks or suitability, your innate preference is inwardly demanding that you only consider certain people, and this negates dramatically your chances for finding a suitable mate that can provide you with the security and friendship that you seek.

Love is then showing itself to be more dependent on you and how you feel than it is any other factor. If this is true the love you believe in does not exist. The love between two people that you believe in and base your whole life around, is really only a reflection of your innate preferences and choice. For certain reasons only determined by your childhood you are deliberately selecting the people in your life, this choice this pre selection cannot be the foundation for love, only bias and judgement, and categorisation. Even if you develop a certain bond and feelings for the people in your life, that cannot be classified as love when it is dependent on the past. If you have chosen a mate because they remind you of a parent, the love you feel for them must resemble the love you felt for that parent. In other words the choice is from the past and so to must the love originate from there.

Love cannot exist in the past, love can only be present in the here and now. If you try and slide it forward from a previous day it evaporates. You can think of the love you felt for your grandmother when you were small, and when you look at her today the love you feel for her now will be similar to when you were a child. But, the love has matured, has developed, your memories associated with this love are now more extensive and thus the fondness appears to have deepened. But, in truth the love you feel for your grandmother now is not the same as when you were small, for when you were small you were a child, your brain was not yet fully developed, your judgement not as acute, and as a result you could have felt this love for anyone. Now, today you only have the memory of that love to hang onto as grandmother ages and declines. You in truth do not feel the same toward her today as you did when small. It is not because of the increased memories, it is because your mind now cannot accept and appreciate your grandmother as you did when small.

When you are small adults are the nucleus of your life, they seem to give everything, and your sole orientation is upon them. When they laugh you laugh, when they cry you cry, when they sing you sing. This is the magic of childhood. A totally accepting and non judgemental perception. You cannot slide these sensations forward as your grandmother and yourself age, for your brain is developing and changing daily. So the love that you feel for your grandmother today is a reflection if you will of what you experienced with her while you were young. The two of you shared a bond grandma also for a brief moment was taken into your childhood world through your total acceptance of her and resonance to her when these moments occurred. This sensory perception of the child might be the closest thing you have to defining what real love is, but nonetheless it remains within the confines of childhood.

So, one could almost argue in truth that when you make this selection for friends and lovers based on the past you are attempting to some extent to bring memories and experiences from your childhood sensory perception back to life. But, as I have just explained this cannot be done, unless you can revert yourself back into a child. Thus the love you believe you have found today with your spouse, cannot be real or true. Why? Because you chose them based on a past experience which cannot be replayed. Your mind was the key when young to enabling the experience of love, of total acceptance, of total union and oneness with the other. Now in this day and age, with your mind full of facts, and lists of things you need to do, there is no room for emptiness, for acceptance, for just being with grandma, for just being with someone. Now when you are with loved ones you are flat out just communicating effectively without misinterpretation, without conflict, without offending or humiliating the other. Now, your mind has forgotten what it is like just to be here in this moment. Now your mind has forgotten how to play, how to let go, how to have fun, and laugh at small simple things. Without this, love is not possible.

You may regard the people in your life with high esteem, you may care for them, and become concerned for a time if they are perturbed, disillusioned, depressed, annoyed, and sick or within a crisis, but this care for them, this concern is merely you worrying. You worrying cannot be equated with love. Although you like to think it can, you like it when others worry about you, you like it when others do things for you, when others molly coddle you. Molly coddling is not love. Chasing after others and doing things for them to make them feel better is not love. It is merely you wanting to do what is right, look saintly or not to worry anymore, so in a bid to help yourself to freedom from worry you set about attempting to fix the situation.

This molly coddling is not love, and most of the feelings you now experience for the people in your life is more molly coddling than it is love. It does not matter how many times you say 'I love you' it does not matter what extremes you go to to prove this love, the desire to please another and be with another is not love. It does not matter how much you miss someone that does not necessarily equate with love. When your favourite TV show halts for the season, you miss your favourite characters for a time, is this love? Can missing something be equated with love? If you miss the wage you earnt while young, does that mean you are in love with it?

You miss anything if it has been in your life for quite some time and then suddenly is gone, an old car, the lady who lived down the street, a comedy series, but missing something does not mean you loved it, does it? Missing and loving have long been associated with each other, but this association does not necessarily mean that they are part of the same thing. Most of your psychologists associate love with a whole range of emotions, but love of itself cannot be dependent on any of these feelings otherwise it is more about the feeling and less to do with love.

In truth an autonomous love is very difficult to define, to describe without naming feelings and sensations such as secure, happy, joyous, missing, tenderness, affection, lust, connection and considerateness. This perhaps is how love can be confusing on earth for there are so many ways to describe it, and each has his or her own way. With no one phrase apt to satisfy all the different loves on earth.

The deep affection you feel for the people in your life could be nothing more than your familiarity with them, as familiarity makes you comfortable. When you are comfortable you relax when you relax you feel good, and this is when you come closest to feeling happy. So love and loving feelings must be associated with your own state of mind, your happiness, and your ability to be receptive to those around you.

Understanding your own mind and how it works, and how it interacts with those around you to promote sensations of love and hate must be key to comprehending love. Only when you comprehend what love is can you hope to attain and sustain it for an indefinite period.

To develop your part in love, we must look more closely at how your mind seeks the familiar, seeks to reproduce or avoid feelings from childhood. To do this I must speak in depth about your mind and what it is capable of. Understanding your mind, will help you to grasp necessary concepts about love.

The mind that you rely upon on a moment to moment basis continuously provides you with a steady stream of thoughts. Some thoughts will pass quickly without even seemingly being noticed by you. Others will repeat themselves over and over within your mind throughout the day. You may not notice as you are attending to work. As these thoughts repeat they will start to induce greater sensation within you, as they build, as the amount of the same or similar thoughts increase, it goes to say that they will start creating sensations, bodily, physiological, psychological, all even at times without your awareness.

If you have a recurring thought that you do not like someone or what someone has just said, your minds tendency is to dwell on it, repeat it, analyse it. If they commented on your work, or your clothes, or said something that you disagreed with you may ponder this for some time, then associated thoughts will come in. Similar thoughts about the person, or questions about your work or clothes to see if what the person said was true or not. This could easily lead your mind into thinking about other clothes in your wardrobe, or clothes the other person has worn, or different aspects of your or their work. These thoughts occur without much awareness from you, you are trying not to pay attention to them.

You could possibly dwell on this for a few hours until lunch, or for the remainder of the day depending on what else occurs. Unbeknown to you these thoughts that you are thinking are scraping over a wound that lies within you. And as these thoughts scrape over this old wound, this similar memory from childhood, the feelings stored within this wound are compounded and aggravated. If you take a moment to look honestly at how you are feeling at this point you would see what I am speaking about. Generally however you avoid this, and attempt to keep on working. This means that as the thoughts scrape over the old wound emotion if only a small amount is released.

This emotion will by the end of the day have you feeling stressed, restless, aggravated or depressed. You will then automatically seek to find relief for this feeling by means which you are familiar with. A drink after work, veging out in front of the computer or TV, texting friends, phoning, eating, sleeping, taking something. All these pursuits you have developed to help you avoid feeling. Day after day your mind controls what you do, what you say, not because it is a hidden demon wanting to punish you, but because this is a well worn habit that you have sustained and created within your past.

When you avoid emotion, you are then forced to project it onto others, and this is why love becomes so important to you. Love binds you with others, you are married, you are family, you must do what is right by each other, you must stand by each other, you must molly coddle each other. This is your protection. This means that you will always have people to let off steam with, to distract your attention away from your wounds and feelings. This means you will always have others to blame and look at when you feel out of sort as a result of these feelings.

Love perhaps then may be everything that you say providing you with happiness, joy, content, certainty, tenderness etc, but maybe also is it a device to help alleviate your inner compression of unseen feelings? Keeping it all under the nice heading of love, makes everything seem normal, ok, and congenial. There is no undercurrent of evil that you need to deal with. Labelling relationships under the heading of love promotes their extension and well being. If you labelled them evil, something would perturb you at night, bunching it under the heading of love could be a device to calm you when you sense that relations on earth are not what they are cracked up to be.

Beloved Ones I am Mary, I come forward here to offer you alternatives to your current perception, a perception which is promoting aggression and violence and intolerance on your earth. To free yourselves from these situations you need to begin looking more closely at how your mind controls you for its own betterment. To enhance this we must see through aspects of many of your pinnacles of fortitude, one of them which is love.

Granted this information is uncomfortable, it is disturbing when you really begin to see and appreciate the insidiousness of the mind, and the staples of your society. But freedom cannot be found amongst ignorance and laxity. If you want freedom you must push yourselves up to the peak of the mountain so that you can see clearly, and over the edge if you must to clear your being from the cobwebs that the comfortableness of your life has warranted.

Love needs to be revisited and reviewed. Governments may have begun overhauling the way they do things, the way banks do things, yet this alone is not enough. All of you have a responsibility to awake your mind, to free it from the prison that is just so comfortable to you, yet which stabs you in the back with the maliciousness of greed, and jealousy, a me or them attitude, injustice and inconsiderateness towards those you do not deem lovable, or capable of giving you love.

Because projection is such a large part of the goings on within your mind, I will devote a full section to it, to help you see through its mechanisms and ways more fully, so that you will have a greater ability to see, recognise and sustain a genuine love.

Maya

Chapter Three – Projection.

Hello my beloved ones once again. Today we speak about projection and all its varied dimensions and guises. Projection is a tool used by the mind to keep you interested in what is happening outside of yourself. It ensures that you remain attached to all you see, hear and do on the outer, and keeps you unaware and in the dark about what is actually happening within you, your emotions, reactions, fears and thought patterns. The mind does this as its aim is survival, the more you chase after the bone it throws the more likely he the mind will remain in control. This is what the mind wants to remain in control.

Yet you have mistakenly thought that the essence of the mind must be you, so following the bone that the mind throws you appears to you to be you staying in control. Just as the dog believes he is tricking you into playing a game with him. But, in reality you are being led and misled by your mind time and time again. It is you could say not entirely your fault that you have allowed the mind to trick you time and time again into blaming your brother or sister for doing things that triggered your emotions, your fears, your biases, beliefs and prejudices. For society has offered few alternatives, few role models who teach and demonstrate how to avoid the pitfalls of the mind, of projection. Few beings on earth at any one time can own up to their own shortcomings, take full responsibility for what does or does not happen in their life, and move forward, inward and upwards.

Nonetheless, once you become aware that many of your assumptions, conclusions, and opinions about others reflect more about you than they do any one or thing else, you will access greater clarity which could see you reversing this dynamic. This dynamic occurs because the beliefs you contain within your mind want to be seen, so they thrust themselves up and out, it is automatic, you do not even know you are doing it, it is a mechanism of the mind, for the mind needs to unburden itself of luggage as often as it can to keep it working to its optimum. The mind appears endless, like a computer it can store thousands of images, memories, facts, data, etc yet every single image or memory, or portion of data is linked to one, two or three main beliefs that you have held since a small child.

Yes it is true, everything within in your mind is connected to these inherent beliefs, and so each piece of data reflects to you an aspect of these beliefs. The data which most strongly correlates to the beliefs in your mind will be more easily remembered and called up. Those pieces of information which are bereft of strong connection to one of your beliefs will be much more difficult to recall. So as omnipotent as the mind appears to be when you break its mechanisms up, you can discover quite real and simple processes which make the mind much less mysterious.

Your brain is highly perceptive, and intelligent, I am not attempting to take away the pure majesty and eloquence of any of the minds capabilities. I am only simplifying it to make it easier for you to see how much you play a part. The inherent beliefs within your mind are tickled if you like every day, by the things that you see, feel, hear, touch, taste and smell. When a sensation has a strong connection to a belief the effects can have a volatile effect. This is however, the mind doing you a favour, trying to bring to your awareness these beliefs and issues, as even the mind knows on some level these beliefs need freedom. Yet, it too is frightened of losing control, and so mixes everything up with random thoughts, feelings, images, impressions which make the whole process wearing and tiring. Leaving you little space to feel, to know, to see.

The mind thus continues to project onto others certain personality traits that you or it are not fond of, so that instead of having to look at why you do not like these traits, you can simply judge the other, hold the other in contempt. This process appears to enable you to get on with life, quickly and efficiently. You do not have to spend years on the therapists couch, you do not have to succumb to feelings that make you feel vulnerable and out of control, you do not have to trust anything, you just get back to life, you watch TV, surf the net, talk on the phone, work, tidy up, drink and sleep and pretty soon you have forgotten all about it. This is efficient, this saves time, energy, and prevents a river of torment and sadness that exists within you from surfacing. This enables you to function well enough to get through each day, get to work, get home from work, communicate with loved ones, and do what has to be done, without as much fuss, drama and despair.

But, sooner or later things start to leak out, you begin to get sensations that you are not coping, that you cannot cope, that you hate your life, your husband, your boss, you get bogged down with negativity despite your best attempts to avoid it, even though you are still projecting onto others all the things you do not want to look at within yourself. So, in truth you end up suffering on both sides, inside, and outside, as after time, all the beliefs and the images and data that your mind stores in relation to these beliefs starts to weigh you down. The longer they remain, the more they grow, the more luminous they become, soon you begin to see things in your dreams, and even sleep does not provide respite. Then you become an insomniac, you cannot sleep, as even here are you becoming disturbed and disrupted. There is no solution. You have no freedom from thoughts of saying the wrong thing, doing the wrong thing, making a bad decision. Or alternatively, you see what is wrong in the world, the injustices, everyone is out to get you or someone else. Everywhere you look something is wrong. Everything in life starts to reflect this, your children are naughty, selfish, impolite, or bully's, your brothers and sisters are telling you what to do and how to do it, everywhere you go people are looking at you frowning at you, annoyed at you, in moments you cannot get away from this sensation that you have sinned, you are wrong, God is wrong, the politicians are wrong, and that you are bad, you have done something horribly wrong. Then life simply becomes a dog eat dog world.

This is what you have created, this is what you are creating, are buying into on a day by day moment to moment basis. You cannot see it clearly because your mind won't give you accurate perception unless you demand it from it. Instead are you left to feel the consequences of your projections coming back to bite you in the butt. For every feeling you project onto someone else, two will project back onto you. This is why all of you feel so alone, so misunderstood, so fed up, so tired, so annoyed and unsure and confused. The only way to rectify this is to start to look at the way in which your mind tricks you into projecting your feelings onto others. Then once you can see this clearly, once you can see why your mind does this, you will be more willing to use tools and methods to ease projection if not prevent it all together.

I assure you, you can ease up the effects of projection, you can enable an honest perception which chooses to look at feelings regularly so that they do not need to be thrown up and out onto others. This method of taking time each day just to look at your feelings, to own them, to see how they connect with certain beliefs you carry, is one of the most potent healing modalities that you have available to you in this day and age.

I know in this day and age my Beloveds are you bombarded with so much conflicting material that at times it is hard to decipher between accurate and inaccurate information. I know that you have so little time left in your day that to think about abstract ideas is the least of your concern, it is at the bottom of the list of priorities. But, tell me Beloved Ones what will happen if you do not think about this? What will happen to you? What will happen to your loved ones and your relationship with them? Even now you must see and recognise how tense some of your relationships have become. You are angry with each other, the other has hurt you, betrayed you, let you down, someone is angry with you, yelling at you, preaching to you about what you should be doing for them, and what you haven't done. Surely, all this blame, all this hostility, all this suppressed hostility so that you can be polite, and seem sane, and on top of things is taking its toll. Surely then, you can see the benefit of seeing clearly through projection, and how precious this would be to all of your relationships, let alone your own peace of mind and sense of worth.

I know this vessel may be making this up, you cannot be 100% sure that she is not, and that is about all the evidence you need to reject this notion and its implications. As I am not in the body, how can I transmit through a vessel, how can you be sure the vessel is not contaminated, influenced? These are reasonable questions, but why I ask do you doubt me and my abilities, yet question the thoughts and games of your mind so rarely?

You trust the thoughts in your mind as if they are God himself, you run and chase after the bone day after day after day with little if any evidence that these thoughts are even real or justified or accurate. But, I in one fowl swoop attempt to help you see beyond the mind, and suddenly you are unsure whether this source can be trusted? Who is controlling who? Isn't your mind the greatest dictator you are ever going to encounter? Yet, so cunning it takes the people time to realise what is going on, and still many dictators have massive supporters and followers as there are those who want and need to believe. I am not asking you to believe, I am asking you to try and see for yourself, work with the exercises and the methods that I provide and see for yourself if I can be trusted and of value. Once you can reach up to the top of the brick wall with one hand, and from there lever yourself up so that just your eyes can see over, will you experience and know with certainty my value and worth. Freedom from the mind, and the ability to redirect ingrained patterns of behaviour is more liberating than winning tatts, meeting the hottest celebrity, or even being a rock star. Trust me, of this you can be certain.

Projection is a reflection of your need to maintain equilibrium within yourself. If you are to suddenly look at something which has bothered you, suddenly then a whole gate opens whereby a waterfall of emotion can tumble down into you at any moment. This is what you are afraid of anyway. You don't like to be seen as negative, or emotional, upset or unable to cope. You want to show people that you are able to cope, that you have got yourself together and that you are a valuable person in the community. Someone who can offer help to others in need, in crisis. Even though this is what you want to uphold, even though you do believe this, does not make it true, correct or necessary. I am here to tell you to let go, allow what needs to surface to surface. Stop holding yourself together, stop trying to be a saint, stop being polite and nice, and helpful. Let go, stop meeting other people's needs and start to look at yours. When you feel angry stop, go to the toilet if you have to and look inside, go inside and look at the anger. You are allowed to be angry at someone who was rude to you, you don't have to make excuses for them. You are allowed to be sad when things are hard or not going according to plan, let yourself be sad, be glum, rejoice in being glum, be so glum and gloomy and miserable that you feel empowered by it, inspired by it, invigorated by it. Throw yourself into it head first, you are standing on a very high diving board and glum is the pool of water below. Dive head first. Swim in it, bathe in it, float in it, hold your breath underwater in it. Do somersaults in it. Love it, cherish it, be it.

How can celebrating gloominess be anything but liberating? You have spent your whole lives running from it, avoiding it, shunning it. Just BE Glum. Stop looking at other miserable people, and characters on TV who you pity, and whine at. Just let yourself be glum. You have my permission to be glum, to be sad, to be upset, and angry and whatever else you want to be, and if others don't like it tell them to stop projecting. You have my full permission. You will never be free of it until you delve into it, love it, want it, enjoy it. Cry until you laugh, be short with people, be blunt, be depressed and inconsolable, just let yourself be upset at this miserable life that forces you into holes that you do not like and which don't like you. Celebrate the disappointment of not getting what you want, let yourself feel angry and pissed and disheartened and afraid all at once. Let yourself be cranky, and in a bad mood, and it just doesn't matter who knows or cares. You have my permission to be honest with your feelings, to explore them and feel them and express them in whatever way you wish.

This may be dangerous you are thinking you may lose the love of loved ones, you may get into trouble, you may lose your spot in your little hierarchy of lovable people, yet if you do not everything you have will and must disintegrate at some point. For it is built on shaky ground, whether you divorce, your child becomes a teenager and gets involved with drugs, whether your sister gets sick, your brother commits suicide, or whether your father goes bankrupt due to gambling, somehow, someway you are going to lose out. When that day comes, and it has the potential to come every day, in small ways, medium sized ways, and big ways, you are going to go into shock. You are not going to know what to do. You will be catatonic, you will go into a coma, even though you are still walking and eating, and sleeping and working. A mist will fog over you, and this mist you have termed depression. If not this you will become anxious nervous, afraid, you will slowly be eaten up by paranoia and all that this entails. There is no escaping the devastating impact of not looking squarely at your feelings and emotions.

Emotional dishonesty is more deadly than cholera in third world countries, more debilitating than a global financial crisis, more severe in its consequence than a multitude of tsunami's or earthquakes. Why, you might query is this so? My response is because this can so easily go undiscovered and dealt with. If you are young and you are unwilling to look at how you are feeling, by the time you reach your mid forties if you have not sought to find ways for inner contemplation and introspection, the chances are in the favour that you never will. Too many patterns of behaviour would have been put in play within your mind, and you will be just so accustomed to relying on the patterns and games of your mind that to change them would indeed take a grand effort and persistence. Not to say it cannot be done, but certainly it will take more from you than *your younger counterparts who have been forced into emotional honesty at a younger* age.

Thus I urge you to consider my plea to you as worthy of your contemplation and reflection it is not for nothing that you are reading this, and whether you believe in synchronicity or not, this moment in time can be life changing for you if you allow it to.

Why wait for heartache? Why wait for more disappointment to change your ways? Look inside now and feel how you are feeling, if you do you can be assured that there is a part of you no matter how small that resonates and feels good and at ease with this material. I am not here to convince you of the need for inner reflection, I am here to help you see your own inner desire and yearning for it. There is a difference, without you I can do nothing.

So fear not, I cannot brainwash you, deceive you, or even pull the wool over your eyes as I will be referring you inwards in each section, what better guarantee can you have that I am working with you and for you, and not for my own agenda or means. I am not here to gain money, what could money possibly give me? Remember I am not in the body? What will I swindle you out of your soul so that I can sell what is left to the devil? Why would I do this when I know he does not exist? What possible reason could I have to bring this information forward than to assist you, assist the earth to move forward , assist your species to move forward in a beneficial direction? Surely if anything was my motivation it would be this? I am connected to you, and you are connected to me, what you can harness helps me, and what I can harness helps you. I am not interested in anything else but to see you move beyond the pain, the regret, the torture of boredom, and restlessness, aggravation and fear that most of you live with. Of this you have my word.

Even this, even your doubt about whether I am real or not, accurate or not is a subtle form of projection. Right now you may not doubt, while reading this you may feel convinced but afterwards your mind will attempt to sway you with doubt, and uncertainty, practical thinking etc Of this you can be assured, you have no escape from your mind and its need to control and exploit you. The fact that it will attempt to coerce you into doubting me is a sign that this information has made it afraid. Turn to it and face it squarely in the face, and ascertain that you are the one with the ultimate control, not the whimsical thoughts that pass through it.

Begin to take time each day to look at your emotions, watch your thoughts, feel your feelings, when someone irritates you, stop as soon as you can, go to your car or the bathroom, and just let the emotion run over you. Look at it and watch it, take yourself inside your centre as you do so, focus on your stomach area and pierce inside this area, and you will begin to see more clearly your emotions and the thoughts behind them. You need do nothing but look at them, you do not need to analyse them and figure out why they are there. Just look at them and feel them. Be angry, be upset, give yourself the freedom and the right to explore your emotions and own them. Stop avoiding, stop projecting them onto others and other situations, just let them be there and you will start however slowly to heal. Do this every day, twice a day if you can, and you will start to feel better about whom you are. You will start to be moved by outer situations and people less, you will be able to let go of petty arguments and ideas much more easily, and you will become more centred on a greater meaning and purpose, that which is and surrounds your growth, development and evolution. There is no cause more important than this.

Know that as you do this, that I and my brothers of light are with you, Sananda, Mechelzadek, Kuthumi, Lord Ashtar, Maitreya and Bartholomew. You can call on any one of us during this time and you can be assured we will be there. Stop looking for signs or indicators, proof that we are there, and just feel, relax, let go and trust that as I am telling you this it must be so.

If you can do this for 5 minutes twice a day, within a week you will feel lighter, happier and more at ease. If you can extend the second session to 15 minutes you will notice even more profound receptivity within you to us and our vibrations, and have a deeper sense of your connection to us, and what we represent. If you can bond with us now in this way, through this simple step, that anyone can do, is not hard or arduous, you will have begun a practice which if sustained will put you in good stead for the remainder of your days. Forget enlightenment, forget perfection, just take this one small step with us, on a daily basis, and I assure you that you will be forming a bridge that will see you through a torrent of disappointment and heartache that may surface in your life. Regardless of what happens in your life, no matter how out of control it appears at times, your steadfastness and ability to connect with us, will make all the difference. The more you work to build this bridge to us now, when everything in your life may appear relatively calm, the more secure the stepping stones you will have to us and our sanctuary in your time of need and crisis.

Even more secure than super, and savings, a house, or a committed relationship, will our union prove invaluable to you as you walk through life and beyond. Trust this, trust us, work with us, and go within on a daily basis. Feel your feelings, and many things will come to you to assist and nurture the development of this connection. Regardless of the decisions you make, and path your life takes, this connection keeps you upright on an invisible path that you cannot see, decide upon or deliberate about, but which you trust is there, even when you don't know where you are putting your foot.

We will develop this connection more so within the next section, please work for a few days before continuing with this practice of inward watching.

I assure you this is necessary, essential, and the best thing you can do for your health, your well being, your development and your relationships.

Trust it is I Mary, I come with love in my heart for you, and a sense that together we can accomplish the seemingly inconceivable, of this you have my word.

In Love and Light my blessed Beloveds, know that you are loved so deeply, nothing you may think or do, makes the slightest mark against it.

You are in my Heart...............

Mary

Maya

Chapter Four - Stopping Projection

Beloved Ones it is I Mary,

I come forward here again to help you transform your love into something more valuable, alive, real and effective within your lives. Currently your love is weak, unkempt, scavenous and lousy as you are used to using it merely as some form of currency to get you what you believe you want and need, and to help others to get what it is they believe they need. This cannot continue forever and a day – it simply will not do, already you can see the price that you pay for this ineffective, measured, and cohersive love. Your children are becoming more and more demanding and trialling stronger and stronger addictions in a bid to find the boundaries, the enticements, the rules of this love, and to break free from them as they have felt the bitter side of this love, this love which is ego centric, shallow, only available to those who do the right thing.

Now is the time to redecorate your love, renovate and clean it up so that it can have a real and lasting effect and value in your lives. To do this you must stop using love as a currency, you yourself must stop the compulsion within yourself to demand love from others, to expect them to do the right thing so that they can earn this love. You must stop yourself from making rules, that either prove or disprove that someone loves you, it doesn't matter if they get home late, or if they do not do what you have asked them to, if they look at another woman, another man, if they forgot to get the milk on the way home from work, if they are too tired to do dishes, if they want to go fishing rather than the movies, if they don't want to go out for dinner with your friends, if they do not want to give grandma a kiss, all these expectations and demands must cease if you want to revolutionise and reinvigorate your love. As you are, you will only continue to hate each other, despise each other for the things that the other has made you feel. But, the time has come where you must own your own emotions, and only through doing this can you begin to grasp or even glimpse at the type of love of which I am speaking. If you get angry at your spouse for coming home late and not calling, or not answering your texts, you have to see and to know that this is your anger – it does not and cannot belong to your spouse, and you have no right of passage to want to make them angry just because you are. If you feel angry no matter for what reason the anger comes from within you and you alone must acknowledge and admit this. The anger belongs to you, the sadness belongs to you, the pain, the heartache and the disappointment all belongs to you. Your society has overdosed on victimhood and it is time to redirect this energy into something more positive and worthwhile.

Of course it is easy to assume that if your husband had of answered your text message that you would have not gotten so angry so it would not be there, but this is not so, the anger is there within you waiting, and the circumstance, your husband being late was only the trigger that enabled it to surface. In truth your husband has done you a favour, you are so in the habit of wanting to ignore all your emotions and feelings that you will do almost anything to distract yourself from them. But thankfully you have husbands and children, and they without question force you to look at how you feel. If you do not things will only escalate and build until you experience even greater heartache, or emotion, as this energy, these emotions need their freedom, and you need them to be released.

Thus, be grateful to your husband when he comes home late and ignores your texts, as he has shown you how angry and upset you can get when you do not feel heard or listened to. Be grateful to your children when they do not listen for they are showing you that you harbour much anger, resentment and pain within. The sooner you can stop yourself from blaming and aggravating the situation by attempting to control every little thing that happens, and just stand back and feel your emotions the better off you and your entire family will be. This is how you prevent projection, you feel your feelings, you take responsibility for how you feel, and you do not attempt to make others responsible for the emotions that have surfaced within you. If the emotion comes it is not coming from the outside, from the circumstance, from your husband, or children or friend, or boss, it is actually coming from you.

If you had been taught at a young age to go within and to make time to sit with and feel everyday what is going on within you, you would already know this, I would not be telling you something you don't really know or understand. But, as your society has not taught you this, as you have only been instead taught that love is a currency that you manipulate the people in your lives with, of course then it is difficult to see what I am attempting to convey. Thus I offer this book, I do not expect you to know already what I am speaking about, although you may have heard about this in the past, still you have had trouble with truly grasping its essence and value. Thus, I come forward here, to not only show you where you are making your mistakes but how also to correct them.

This will take some effort and work on your part, but it will be minimal compared with the effort, the time, the energy it takes to distract yourself from these emotions everyday day after day. Everything that you are currently doing, particularly in your spare time, is a result of not wanting to look at and acknowledge these emotions. Even the enormous amount of work that you do, you do not so that no one call you lazy, but so you do not start to feel the restlessness, the anxiety, the nervousness of when these emotions begin to stir. You do not want to have to look at them, you do not want to have to feel their consequence, as they are painful, they will bring emotion and it will not be pretty. Thus, as you have become so skilled at not looking at these they then must manifest in your life, so that you can feel and get more in touch with what is happening within you. When they say that you are creating everything in your life, and that your thoughts are creating your life, this is what they mean. Normally it is not your conscious thoughts, the thoughts you allow yourself to see that are creating your life, just because you think you want to win a million dollars does not mean that this will manifest, as you have other more volumous and potent thoughts that have been magnetised with your emotions that are undoing your best intentions from within.

Until you free these thoughts and emotions are you then a slave to them, they will create trauma and heartache in your life time after time after time. When the global consciousness has supressed too much of these thoughts, emotions and energies and they then have nowhere to go, they too will then start to create mishap and mayhem in your global village. It is not that difficult to understand, it is simple physics, what goes up must come down, if you continue to supress and ignore how you truly feel the world you live in will force you to feel and see them all at once amidst horrific circumstance if need be.

This is not a punishment from God, this is not happening to you as some karmic debt, this is a simple matter of physics, you are choosing to try and hold down energies that want to be set free, how long you can hold them down for may be quite substantial, but certainly will not be indefinitely. Like trying to hold down an extra-large helium balloon all by yourself, once you take your eyes off it for a second or a strong current of wind comes you will have little chance.

All of you know this, you have all heard of this theory somewhere throughout your life you know or have heard conversations about how you are all supressing your feelings, yet to actually work at setting them free is quite a difficult task. It is difficult as you want to have someone to blame, it is so much easier to blame someone else when you feel hurt, betrayed, or undervalued, their actions may seem deserving of your blame, but unfortunately for you this is just your habit of projection. It is nothing more and nothing else, it is pure habit on your part. Habit as you know is not easy to change, but you must attempt to work with it here, otherwise the ultimate price you will pay within your life could be quite devastating and shocking, and no amount of projection will save you.

If you can see or even feel how giving up projection can heal your version of love, can purify it and make it more welcoming, authentic and permanent, you may be able to find enough momentum within you to persevere with this idea. This is ultimately what you need to do, this will heal most of your dysfunctions and ailments on earth. If you can work with this one idea of not projecting your own emotions onto others no matter how wretched their actions have been, you begin to change the dynamic of blame and persecution on the earth. If you can help humanity do this, if humanity could grasp the necessity of this notion or concept, if they could work with it wholeheartedly there would then be little need for many of your current devices or services to help deal with the consequences of this phenomena.

Your mental health rates would decrease, if people are not being unnecessarily blamed it will reduce tension within relationships, it would make relationships more valuable, effective, supportive, positive, enlivening and comforting in your times of need. As opposed to currently where people are feeling so out of touch with one another, so unloved and uncared for as they have been misinterpreted time and time again as people can only see what exists for them not others. When you project your emotions onto others, when you place your sole emphasis on having people in your life love you, and do what you require to feel loved, you create a bubble which is constantly seeking this sanctuary or stability offered by this sense of feeling loved by others. Thus do you all then become so focused on receiving love from others, that it becomes more difficult to detect when someone may need love, comfort, to be heard or seen by you. It is no fault of your own, and many of you who need love from others become the carers who listen and nurture as this buys you your love. Yet, at the same time this outward emphasis prevents you from truly taking the time to notice and to truly care for, to truly hear what the other is saying no matter how good your intentions you will mishear them time and time again as you are focused on getting your love, not giving it.

This has created so many dysfunctions within your lives. This one simple concept has literally alienated you all from each other, and I have for quite some time wanted to help you see your mistake, but I too have been misinterpreted as people need to feel loved and valued by me, that anything else that I may attempt to convey is incomprehensible to them. Thus your mental health concerns which are responsible for much of your crime and corruption would inevitable reduce. This would take time, it would not happen immediately but if your whole community, could work with this one idea – could stop themselves projecting it would begin to reverse the negative dynamics in place which have continued for far too long.

It would take time for people to begin raising families in this way, and you would need to wait until a generation had been raised in this fashion to see its full effects, but even so you would still see magical differences if your community could really cling to and hold onto this concept. Imagine the people suffering with depression, anxiety, loneliness, heartache, the children who feel alienated at home, who have to then act up or out to be seen, the brats that are being raised as parents do not have time to be still as they do not want to risk running into their own feelings and supressed emotions. The crime that occurs when juvenile delinquents are bored and at odds with their parents and want to make their parents pay. They hurt someone, injure someone, kill someone and then that family is irrevocably lost in pain and guilt and heartache affecting them and what they do to others, and what they create within their lives.

This viscous circle just keeps on continuing emitting ripples small at first that gradually grow larger and larger affecting more and more people and communities within their circumference. Now, is the time to see that you do have ultimate power and control over this, you can take responsibility for your actions you can wake up and see the mistakes the very simple mistakes that you are making. Mistakes that can easily be corrected. All you need do is make time each day to go within your being, feel your emotions, tune into your energy and see what is coming up and this will help you to move forward and away from your current crisis.

This will not be easy in the beginning it will take time to get the hang of tuning into your own being and seeing your emotions, or taking time out immediately after a fight or argument or disagreement to see and feel your emotions, to see why this is angering you, annoying you, making you depressed and sad. Yet, if you can practice it, if all of you agree to practice it, if you are in a relationship where you have discussed and agreed upon the value of stopping projection you will more easily be able to undo this. The more you can do this, the easier it will become, and the more likely you will be able to eventually stop yourself projecting, before an argument and be able to then see what wants release from within you, and be able to free your being from it. Even if it is not prior to an argument, even if you have to argue violently first, if you can afterwards tune into why this whole scenario is upsetting you and stay there until you see what it is, you will free yourself from pain and anguish and heartache. If you can see what wants release, if you can sit with it, and allow it to be there, it will evaporate.

Just doing this much will clear your being considerably and give other suppressed energies, memories and trauma's the go ahead to seek release also. This will create a steady stream of surfacing emotions and feelings, and this will at times bring tears, it will at times be painful, it will be uncomfortable, yet the understanding you will gain about yourself and why things are upsetting you, and the freedom and release you will feel once you have seen these suppressed resonances is so mightily wonderful and liberating that you will become even more and more determined to free others within you. You will become hooked on this, for you will begin to feel so light, so free, so clear and wonderful. The dark density that holds you down now will vanish and you will smile for the first time in a very long time, you will feel that this is your authentic smile, and it is.

This my children is why I come – not to warn you of dire consequences if you do not see what I am telling you, but to show you how simple and easy evolution and growth actually are. This whole world can literally transform itself right before your eyes if you are willing to work with these concepts. You have after all nothing to lose, and I Mary validate all that I am speaking about.

Free yourself beloved ones free yourself from the restriction that currently you live amongst. Take heed of my words listen and feel them and think about them, let them penetrate to the centre of your core, be not afraid of what I come to share – be open be willing to walk with me a little for I assure you you have nothing to lose and absolutely everything to gain.

My ideas may seem a little out there at first but once you begin working with them once you start to see and feel their benefit and effect you will understand why I am saying what I am saying and you will see that my words are blessings, not a curse.

Projection does not seem to exist to you because you have not taken the time to look at how you throw all of your emotions onto others – you spend so much time convinced of others wrong doings that you do not have any time left to look at your own shortcomings and choices. Whenever you are upset with someone else you have projected your own emotions, thoughts and issues onto them, there is no other possibility. It is easier for you to blame them, see their faults then it is to recognise and work with your own shortcomings, your own fears, your own desires and needs and demands. When someone does not do the dishes for you it is easier to see how selfish and self centred they are, it is easy to see how they do not appreciate you, how arrogant and animalistic they may be. It is not easy to see that you are putting your own dislike of doing dishes onto them – you are expecting them to love you in a way and form that you dictate. You are seeking to have your needs met through them. It is not the dishes in the sink which is the problem, it is not the fact that you both do not like doing them, it is not the problem that you have done the dishes 5 times this week and they have done them only once, the problem is that you are not feeling heard, you are feeling alone and isolated and unsure so you need someone else to fill the gap, to step up and do the dishes so that at least it appears like someone is listening to you – you may not have control over anything else in your life or being but you have control over that.

In the end it is these miserly attempts at control, and being able to orchestrate the people in your life so it looks like they care for you which is your greatest undoing. To attempt to move people around on the chess board as if they are pawns, to attempt to make yourself feel loved through the actions of others can offer only a second rate feeling of love. It cannot be true love, it cannot be real, it can at best be pretend love. It makes you feel better, all seems to be working for you on the outside, in your life, and that for a time can convince you that things are also ok on the inner.

Yet, this cannot last, the people who you made do the dishes will resent you, and they will seek their vengeance when you least expect it, at another time, when you are out with your friends they will drink too much, say too much embarrass you no end. Then another wound opens up before you and you then have to seek even greater control over this person to enable the sense of love to continue and for you to feel nourished and whole. You are teetering on the edge, on the brink of meaninglessness, and you seek to establish your needs in every aspect of your life, so that you do not have to feel or acknowledge or see this void, this grand canyon of hopelessness and sense of not being loved.

Only when you can see this canyon, only when you can be honest with yourself and your life will you be able to let projection go. When you can see that the efforts you have been making to date to help you to feel loved and worthy are not really working are instead only covering over the gap, will you then feel ready to think about things differently and let projection slide out of your mind and your life. In the end it does not matter if your children and spouse do the dishes or not, in the end it does not matter if they are selfish or not, in the end it does not matter if they are pig headed, arrogant, impolite or greedy, for all these attributes are theirs not yours, and you have no need to fuss and bother with them. What you should be concerned about is your own inner health and wellbeing. If trying to force the pig headedness out of your husband or children is driving you witless, why continue? Just let them be, just let it all be as it is – all you need do is forsake the opinion of others, and the need to be esteemed in other people's eyes. If you can let this go, you will naturally feel better about yourself and won't necessarily demand so much of the people closest to you.

If you can offer yourself this freedom, if you can offer this freedom to your spouse and children, if you can simply sit with this feeling of not being loved and not have to try and correct or fix it you will with time get used to it, and it will get used to you. You will see within you that you are not feeling unloved because of anything that your children or spouses are doing but from something that happened within your childhood or even a past life. It is not up to your husband and children to correct the mistakes that perhaps your parents unwittingly made, or someone in a previous life, in truth what lies in the past cannot be fixed, it can only be accepted.

When you can see how these impulses from the past are deluding you, and making you feel less then when in truth they have absolutely no power – you will be amazed at how easily you can release and correct your misperception. Letting these impulses go is all that is required, and then naturally you are going to feel better with the spouse you have chosen and with how your children have turned out. All the mechanics of child rearing all the do's and don'ts hold little weight when you are at peace – for your state of mind will greatly impact and effect your children.

Everyday life has a way of complicating even the tiniest of things – this is what makes going within difficult and tiresome – of course most of you will give up, will turn and run, but when you have had your break and you feel better there is no reason not to return. Learning about concepts like this will be essential as you move forward into this century and decade, for you as a species will not be able to move away from the problems and despair that currently you live with until you do.

Technology may assist you to communicate and connect with each other, but it is not aiding you to become a more aware and considerate species. At present your technology is being used to fuel greater violence and mistrust, certain acts are viewed worldwide and this incites greater violence, difficulty and hate. To move beyond this it is essential that you begin in your home and life to bring balance back, one way to do this is to see how projection affects and destroys all that you are working towards. When you can see what is really happening when you project your own emotions onto others when you can see how this is a blatant avoidance of your responsibility, when you can integrate ways to move beyond this within your own life, you will see that change is possible and not only this change is beneficial.

You can create a more loving, stable and connected home life for you, your spouse and your children just by adding a few small details to your everyday, and by hopefully taking away a few obligations which you feel are overall not in everyone's best interests. You then create greater time just to be in nature, just to be in your home, just to be with each other. The first thing, however, is to want to be with each other – and to attain this you need to surrender to each other, listen, enjoy and take time with each other. You need to allow yourself to be vulnerable and naked with those who are closest to you, you need to be able to share your fears, your secrets, your wishes and longings. This is what creates intimacy.

It is difficult to be close with one another when you are all rushing around trying to get ready to go out and play sport, go to a dance class, choir etc etc Too many activities on your agenda only highlights your mistrust of each other and your desire to not be with them – to turn this around you need to sacrifice an activity, going out socialising with friends perhaps so that you can spend time together as a family. Then when you are together you need to trust each other, share with each other, and the parents need to set the example here, if you cannot be open and trusting with your children why should they with you?

This is all about bringing balance back into your life, and creating a firmer footing for your relationships so that you can express your true feelings rather than having to project them on to those you care most about. This then becomes the priority, start making time for family, even if that is just spending 10 minutes talking openly with each child up in their bed before they go to sleep. Explain to them why you said what you said and did what you did, explain to them that you are feeling stressed and confused and unsure. Let them see that you are human, be vulnerable, let them see your flaws, it will endear you to them. It will not push them away, it will not devalue the respect that they have for you, it will not make them think less of you, it will open an energetic space within your relationship with them so that honesty and feeling can be more easily expressed.

This is what you need in your life if you are a parent, and this is what your children need also. When you are bombarded with so much screen time, so much irrelevant information streaming live to you each moment, you then have to stop and reassess your day, you have to stop this insidious current of information and make deliberate time for one on one time, for honesty and vulnerability. This will help to relieve your stress, it will create greater bonds between you and your children, and it will give you a better sense of what authenticity is. For my dear ones you are losing contact with this quicker than you are losing contact with nature.

The good news is the more you allow these seemingly small and insignificant moments into your life, the more they will grow and multiply all by themselves. If you can work with this idea, if you can make deliberate time for those who you live with each day, for the next two weeks, and if you can keep it up, within the two week period you will see that these moments have grown to more than just one a day. This is good news my friends, good news indeed, almost as if there is an invisible force helping you to regain authenticity and balance back into your life. Work with this – if you can work with nothing else that I share, work with this dear ones and you will be rewarded, you have my word.

Creating time and space for true communication with those whom you love dearly is a real and potent force which not only can counteract the enormous load of irrelevant dry, and monotonous information you get through the screen, it balances your energy out, makes you feel better, more confident, less stressed, more aligned and in harmony with life, as humans seek human interaction, this is how children thrive, on human interaction and care, so too adults, human interaction and care. A simple equation, but somehow the formula has been lost amongst the confusion and deliberate laxity of your everyday, modern lives. Now is the time to reverse this, now is the time to put you and your children and your spouse, first, forget about achievement and glory and success, these things are not real, they cannot sustain you, they cannot alleviate stress, as they are only ideals in your head, notions, fantasies, fiction, for even if they do eventually come into play after much hard work, they will not come in the way you expect, and will not offer you the freedom, pride, love and care that you think it will.

Why should you believe that these things can offer you love when love awaits you right in this moment within an interaction with your child, your spouse, your parent or friend? Being vulnerable is the key to feeling loved and supported and cared for – career success is empty and harrowing and not easily gotten, the money spent before you have even earnt it. Face the fact dear ones, love is yours for the taking right now – it is an apple and you are in an apple orchard – you do not need more, you simply need to know how to pick the apples. To pick the apples you become vulnerable, you express how you truly feel to those you feel closest to.

This is how you bring an authentic love back into your life, this is how you start to reverse the dynamic of the polluted love that you have enslaved yourself to to date. This is how you make sure everything that I say about your love is out dated and incorrect. Prove me wrong, work with this and show me, parade it around for all to see, how glorious and satisfying you have made this human love. Make it more than what it is, make yourself more, dive into the love that you have as if it were a submerged cave, dive and dive deeply, nourish it, revere it, and put it absolutely before work, before money, before power and greed and the need to show off, the need to have it all, the need to keep up with the Jones's.

At the end of the day, even if you can start to work with this idea, you will be unable to continue with it, someone you love will slap you in the face, will turn their nose up at this new form of love, and this will throw you off guard back into old patterns old rhythms. Then life will eat up the rest of your good intention with busyness, obligation and the screen. So my window of opportunity to influence or assist you is small, thus I urge you even if just for two weeks to work with this idea, regardless of what happens after this work with this idea.

If you can you will be able to more readily work with other methods and ideas that I bring forward.

If you really want to work with this idea in a more solid way that is going to have more permanent affects you need to see the necessity of giving up projection. You need to breed an honesty back into your being about your feelings, you need to be able to accept them and take responsibility for them, this is why my last suggestion is valuable. Remember, I am here to offer you many paths so that you can choose the one that you feel the best with, all of you are different and need to work with these ideas in your own way and time, thus I am providing a plethora of methods so that none of you have the excuse that this method did not work for me. The methods work, your intention and dedication is the only variable.

To be honest about your emotions and feelings is one of those grey areas on earth where you never really know how it will go down with others. Unless of course you are on a therapists couch where all of a sudden you do not know what to say. Your species has been overtaken with intelligence, knowledge, the need to know, thus facts have been given high precedence within your modern day lives, facts and sport generally have taken over, the arts, music, poetry have smaller followers and are slowly being overtaken by more convenient expressions of emotion such as partying and getting drunk. Thus, is your society paying a price for this choice, and many of you are suffering as a result.

The reason for this growth in the intellect and knowledge based fields and the pure neglect within the art type fields obviously comes back to money. People all of you need to make a living, and everyone knows that it is not profitable to be an artist, unless you are the cream of your crop. Thus, has knowledge taken over as it is the main highway towards earning a living. Of course you want your children not to have to worry about money so you guide them down the path of least resistance to become high earning business people, lawyers, doctors, managers etc Parents really only support the artistic or musical path as a means of compromising with their children or patronising them until they come to their senses. Some see a path through which this can become a viable living and thus support this, but generally overall this is not supported.

Without art, and creative expression within your lives it leaves little to the imagination as to why you are all so stunted and isolated, suppressed and angry. You are making your society more and more robot like, machinelike, set like concrete and the choices to vary this pattern is quickly diminishing. Thus, for those of you who enjoy the intellect, who do not have an artistic bone in your body you seem to get along reasonably well, you enjoy this lifestyle that to some extent seems to have been designed and choreographed just for you, your preferences, likes and dislikes.

But you are still paying a price, although you may be unaware of it creative expression appreciating the finer things in life assists you also to feel more alive, connected and nourished. When life is just grey, when life is nothing more than facts and figures, when every day is the same, when you lose your contact with your environment, when you lose your appreciation for nature, then a very sad and deflating phenomenon occurs. You begin to close down to life, your senses begin shutting down even without your awareness – creative people will feel the effects of this more vividly – but all people will suffer. You become dull or blunt to life, you become immune to its greyness, its boring facts and figures, you lose enthusiasm for life, you lose joy and good heartedness, you lose your ability to want to involve yourself in anything, you lose your ability to want to inject yourself into things. Slowly slowly you begin shutting down – you start to not notice what is happening in your life, you focus on your work, on the screen, this is what gets you by. You become more and more encased into this ritual of following the same boring pattern day after day, month after month, year after year. Nothing changes even when you desperately want it to change. Nothing changes. You have cut yourself off from life, and from living, from expression and creativity, from nature and nurture, what else then is left?

Then you only have your addictions to cure you, to make you feel alive when all along you are feeling bereft of feeling of care, of substance. So those with no creative impulse begin to fantasize about the young girl at work, they may even pursue her, dreaming up all possible ways that they could court her, touch her, be with her. They crave pornography, sex with young prostitutes, sex, affairs, anything that will help them to feel alive again, young again, involved again. There is no way out for all of you- you have painted yourself into a corner. You have year after year after year closed down your expression, your creativity, your interaction with nature, you have isolated yourself from those in your life, as relationship was too painful, too confronting.

Now like a dried up old leaf do you sit and read this and wonder what I am speaking about, you cannot see the part even now that you have played in your life, that has forced you to shut down, and to admonish only fact, only maths, only science, only what can be proven. You believe that this way of life is normal, it is the status quo, there is nothing else, but my dear ones you have been deceived, for there is more, much more. Now is the time, to re open your centres to life, now is the time to re-open your connection to the earth and to each other. If you can do this, you may just be able to reverse this dry brittleness that is slowly invading your lives and replace it with young, fresh, juicy love and care. Even if you are old it is not impossible, even if you think you are well and truly past it, you are not, you can make a difference in this life and within your being. All you need is better know how, and many things easily can be resolved and transformed.

The way forward from here is to reopen your heart centre back up, re open your life back up, re open yourself up to life. Before you can successfully do this however you will need to stop projecting your emotions onto others. This will affect your ability to truly open to life, it will create aggravation within you and will inhibit you from seeing what you need to see to be at peace. Peace is after all perception, you can easily attain it once you understand the triviality of the thoughts within your mind. To understand the thoughts in your mind you need to own them, be comfortable with them and be ready to let them go. If you do not even know that they are there how can you let them go?

Stopping yourself from projecting your own feelings onto others will call for discipline and restraint when you are dealing with them – it will also call forth perseverance and tenderness from within you. You will need to be kind with yourself as well as others – if you cannot be gentle with yourself then you will be unable to do as I ask and if you unable to do as I ask you will still project your emotions onto others. Inhibiting your own ability to move forward and free yourself back into life.

If you genuinely want to stop projecting onto others you must get into the habit of recognising and seeing your own emotions and thoughts – to do this you must carve a pattern of going within each day to see what is coming up within you and to recognise and understand what you find there. This appears boring and unnecessary to you now, but once you begin to work with it and get into the swing of it you will come to enjoy and look forward to it. You will feel much more in control of your life, and your being, you will be able to set aside moods which may have at one point engulfed you. Knowing that you can sidestep your moods offers a great feeling of power and control over one's life, when one has this, the urge to control others reduces naturally which again enhances rather than detracts from relationship and your feeling of being loved, and being able to offer love.

In this day and age are practices like this going to become more and more relevant and necessary – if you think you are going to get through the remainder of your life without someone suggesting meditation, relaxation techniques, or alternative therapies you are not seeing properly. The time will come when you can no longer deny that you are suffering with stress and when that time comes you will indeed need to consider meditation. Beginning with it now gives you a head start, puts you out in front of the race towards this inevitable practice – more and more as your health declines, as your health systems fail you, as you need to seek alternative therapies to help keep you fit and healthy you will see just how pertinent and necessary this skill is.

I am going to offer you here then an exercise that helps you to get into the habit of tuning into your own energy which will enable you to see what is attempting to surface within you. Doing this regularly will assist you to clear your mind and being from unwanted energies and influences and suppressed memories and emotion. This is where it all starts this is where you either choose to go with this, or back away from it. You have nothing to lose and possibly much to gain, what awaits you within may take time to surface, may need dedication and persistence on your part but assuredly it will come – you have my word.

Please work with the following exercise each day for the next four days:

Tuning In Exercise

Please close your eyes and breathe deeply for a moment or two. Breathe normally and then feel yourself being pulled by some magnetic force into your solar plexus region – the area between your ribs and belly button – and place as much of your consciousness here for as long as you can. Continue to focus on this region and then wait and see what images, feelings, sensations, thoughts or emotions surface.

When something comes up follow it, no matter how hazy or obscure, or even if you think it is just your imagination – follow it to see where it leads – it will become clearer and it should reveal its relevance to you.

If you are having difficulty seeing or sensing anything then please focus on your heart centre for a few moments and sense it spinning and opening and becoming wider – once you have a real sensation that your heart centre is widening and opening go back to your solar plexus region to see if you notice anything here now. Be alert and aware – do not dismiss anything and trust that this process is a natural one that occurs spontaneously within humans as it is one of their inherent gifts.

Now go back to your solar plexus and follow what you notice rising up within you – follow it, ask appropriate questions, remember that I am with you, and see how much better you feel afterwards. When something does surface you should sense or see the relevance of it to your life now, this creates relief within you, as you understand more clearly why you feel the way you do. If nothing comes focus on how you are feeling and just focus here until it starts to loosen and begins emanating energy.

This is a very freeing and liberating exercise when done properly – and you should seek to work with it as thoroughly as you can over the next few days so that you can really harness its potential and opportunity. You cannot expect miraculous things to occur on your first attempt. Give it time, work with it, have patience and perseverance it will pay off in the end you have may word.

Out of all the things you do in everyday life, this pursuit is valued immensely it is a skill that will assist you to walk through life with greater awareness. This is something to aspire towards yes?

Without awareness of what is really happening within you how can you even hope to attain at any type of happiness or sense of peace? While you insist on denying your emotions time and time again so that you can perceive them in others, blame others, and need others are you left to the mercy of a savage universe which may or may not grant you your innermost desires.

To move away from this susceptibility which sees you constantly needing others to help you get in touch with your emotions you need to stop denying how you feel about things. You need to work every day to see what is going on within you and you do this through the exercise that I have just given you. Explore your feelings, and responses to life within – this will open you up to tremendous energy and insight. This will slowly take away the need to deny how you are really feeling and you will be less likely to project them onto others.To enhance this notion within you I will continue to speak about your denial within the next chapter. This naturally follows on and blends with this topic of preventing projection.

What is Love? Messages from Mary on Love and Fulfilment

Maya

Chapter Five – Denial Breakthrough

Greetings again Beloved Ones,

Today is a new day, today you can start over, leave the past behind and know that indeed there is a solid path for you to walk towards your inner being. At the end of the day this is what will matter, this is what will make a difference within your life, this will help you to alleviate many of the traumas and difficulties that currently you live with. Going within certainly is not an easy ask, it will require much patience and steadfastness on your part, but the gifts you will receive as a result are well worthwhile.

The tune in exercise alone, which I have just given you, is a method of practice which will help see you through to the end of your days if you persist with it. If you can work with nothing else that I provide, just being able to do this tune in daily will help you to see what needs to be seen within you and this precipitates their release. Spirituality is not just about altered states or higher states of awareness you need to simultaneously find methods to help you to deal with the glue that exists within you, and to help you overcome it and not give in to it, not get stuck in it.

The vibrations that create who you are respond to direction, respond to awareness but while you continue to ignore them, suppress them, deny them, smother them do you leave them little choice but to smoulder within you like embers waiting for some fuel, more wood, more paper, to help it burn, and it will seek to inflame your life and being as often as it can, as these energies need movement to exist. Without movement they eventually will die out on their own, but they do everything that they can to survive and gather fuel if not freedom and you unfortunately in many instances are the fuel.

You cannot suffocate them, you cannot kill them, just because you keep on smothering them, it actually takes quite a lot for them to perish and you will lose this battle if you think ignoring them will eventually dissolve them. There is no choice you have no option but to release these energies, and to see them for what they are. In the beginning this will be hard, in the beginning this will be difficult, it will make you feel and experience pain, hurt and anger, fear, dread, anguish, self-hatred and persecution, you will undoubtedly think you are going mad at times, and will also think that you cannot continue with it. But these resonances once they are in the habit of being seen and looked at will be set free more easily within you, and this will create momentum in which they can effortlessly begin to leave.

When they leave, and they will, you will be left with a lightness of being previously unknown to you, meditation will become much easier, life will become much easier, you will not get as upset by the trivial goings on in your life, you will be able to offer the compassion and love and receptivity that those in your life and you deserve. This perspective is unreplaceable this perspective is what it's all about. So what if others don't share your vision your purpose, your need for this, it does not mean that it is wrong or foolish just because the multitudes as yet have not discovered its necessity.

You are a pioneer, an adventurer; you are leading the way, for you are grappling with higher states of being, higher awareness, higher vibrations at the same time that you are also working with and transforming lower energies and vibrations. You are a juggler, you are multidimensional. You are carving a deep path to your core, deep and wide enough so that others can easily follow if they choose. This is what is necessary – otherwise you will have to continue to deny your feelings for the entirety of your life. Do you really want to continue in this manner? Do you really want to live this life of denial and consequence? When the option for something much fresher, alive and invigorating does exist? The world is your oyster, you can choose moment to moment what it is you want, and what it is you don't want.

The tune in exercise then helps you to move beyond projection as it day by day introduces you to how you are feeling within. With time and experience you will begin to experience these feelings as vibrations, energies, light, and then this process will become even more invigorating and transformative. Without this process or exercise of attending to your emotions and feelings spiritual work becomes bare and empty. Working on your higher mental and spiritual planes will not affect and influence or transform your lower aspects or parts. Thus if you pursue meditation and heightened awareness without addressing these lower aspects of everyday life, and leave the suppressed energies lying within you, dormant, then any light or higher vibration that you experience or receive within your meditations will be indigestible to you.

Thus many spiritual seekers over the years who have ignored the call of the market place and everyday life and instead solely focused on liberation of mind only, and having fantastical spiritual experiences of bliss and ecstasy, vastness and light become even more unbalanced and off centre within everyday life. They have even greater inability to cope with the rocks that life inevitably throws at them forcing them more and more into greater and greater retreat just to keep their heads above water. They become more and more dependent on others to resolve their everyday dilemmas and this works against them in the end not for them.

In the end this type of approach will thwart the seeker with greater and greater difficulty, meaning that they will continue to supress more and more energies and unresolved issues, feelings and responses to everyday life. This will bog them down more into life, creating a duality whereby they crave the spiritual more so, and cannot be themselves unless flying high in some meditative experience.

This is not our aim here – this is not being offered as some form of escape, meditation alone will not suffice, will not unblock the toilet, will not clear your being of these energies, it will not improve relationships if you are still unassertive and avoidant of expressing taboo emotions such as anger, hatred, greed and selfishness. You must be free to experience and express all types of emotion, and some Buddhist advocates have left many a young novice convinced that to express anger or rage is unspiritual, egotistical or simply unacceptable for a spiritual seeker. Thus forcing many into greater and greater periods of suppression and guilt as a result.

In the end you cannot fool your own soul, you may be able to fool a spiritual guru or leader, a healing practitioner, a teacher, a life coach but certainly you will be unable to convince your own soul. For your soul sees what lay hidden within, and just because you may be good at suppression, certainly many seekers are masters at this, does not mean that you have been let off the hook. Real work must be done, thorough work, both on your lower aspects, and on your higher parts if you wish to concertedly change and transform your being. There are many means and ways of going about this, but certainly the tune in method that I have provided is going to be the staple of your diet within the spiritual feast you crave. Like bread or water, or vegetables, without this tune in exercise you risk losing the value and preciousness of everything else you may witness or experience.

Indeed if you could absorb efficiently all the essential spiritual philosophy within this teaching and others there would be no need for inner work, for releasing suppressed energies – but your ability to be able to do this is to say the least negated – for they like an invisible wall stand between you and your core being, your soul. Whilst you might have inflated, revelatory experiences within your mind, they cannot directly link and anchor into your soul. While these experiences lie outside of your direct connection to your soul, which directly connects you to the greater universal energies, will all your experiences flitter away like pollen seeds in the wind. They will not transform your being, they will not extricate all your bad habits and fears, neurosis and desires into light, or love or pure acceptance and awareness. This simply is not possible, you need real effective methods to release these inner demons so that you can know your soul and through that link your spiritual experiences into your energetic being.

This is why your spiritual pursuits have failed to date, this is why your spiritual endeavour has become de valued and underscored within your society, for it has not had any real and lasting impact on your life and social hierarchy. It has not been able to transmute the fear and the hostility and the lust and greed, and insecurity that all of you hold within, and while spirituality remains an aloof agenda that neither penetrates or resolves psychological issues will you forever be living in a wasteland of plastic and machines, violence, aggression, corruption and pollution.

You need to see spirituality in a new light, you need to see it not only as a means of relaxation, of stress release, of being able to cope with life more readily – nor must you see it simply as some airy fairy irrelevant unbased or unproven philosophy with no real impact or effect for your life. All of you need to begin to see spirituality as a means of healing and restoring you to your full potential, which can be realised and actualised within this life. It means not only being able to go to alternate realms within your mind, it means not only being able to connect more readily with your soul, which most are convinced does not exist, it means being able to harness the full potential of your mind being able to sense and to feel what is happening around you on many levels not just one, it means being able to penetrate into your life more directly ask more appropriate and accurate questions so that you can get more accurate answers, and can clear away the debris of your communication so that you have a clearer understanding and comprehension of why what is happening within your life is happening.

Spirituality takes you to your core, when you are in your core, when you are aligned, you are invigorated, you think more clearly, can concentrate on what is important for longer, you can spot lies, falsities, delusions, time wasters more efficiently. You have a heightened sense of what needs to be done and the quickest and most effective way of getting there. You are ultimately in tune with all of life at once, thus you can see or sense immediately the right course of action. You can appreciate the red lights as a necessity for keeping you in the right place at the right time, you can appreciate forgetting your keys, to slow you down so that you do not miss an important opportunity, you can see and feel and sense why the people in your life feel the way they do, as you are so in tune with your feelings, thoughts, and idiosyncrasies that it is easy to understand, comprehend and relate to others.

This improves the quality of communication within your life, and this will undoubtedly improve your relationships. When you feel nourished by your relationships rather than penned in or condemned by them, you slowly start to open up and trust life, you feel better, you think better, you are more trusting, you are more receptive to what is going on around you, and whether this leads to great and fantastic spiritual liberation or not does not matter, for you are just so content, so at home where you are. This is the ultimate aim of any spiritual philosophy and method. Acceptance of what is is the vehicle through which you develop and nurture compassionate awareness, forgiveness and love. There is and can be no higher ideal than this.

Thus, spirituality is for everyone, and it is essential that you recognise this now and in the future, if you think that you will be able to survive the entirety of your life without adopting some spiritual practice you are either very narrow or very foolish, for you simply have too many people on earth, too many energies both within each individual and the earth for you to be able to avoid trauma without some alternate spiritual practice which helps you to deal more effectively with what life throws in your direction. Thus, spirituality is a necessity, it is not some obscure, out of the ordinary occult, mystical secret ritual or weird obsession. You do not need to dance naked under a full moon, you do not need to cast spells or recite mantras day in day out. It is not about visualising a magnificent future for yourself, it is not about believing in some far off god who obviously does not care about his children, it is not about dogma, commandments, rules and laws, beliefs and a certain moral code. Spirituality is above and beyond all this, spirituality rises above what appears to be so that it can meet each moment as it is and work solidly from here.

If you think that what I mention in this book is not for your immediate assistance on a practical level then you have misperceived my intention – for I can assure you this is not the case. I am here, and have always been here to assist you from where you are – I do not expect you to climb over hills and valleys, and up steep rocky ascents to get to me, I do not expect you to be some type of Edmund Hillary, you do not have to be extraordinary to work with me – you do not even have to be spiritual, a meditation expert or teacher, healer, I am here to help you, the one sitting on your couch with a coffee checking for messages on Facebook or your phone – I am here for you who are about to go pick the kids up from school, who is tired from just clearing the kitchen, working overtime for your boss, I am here for you who are scared and feel all alone, there is no one who truly understands how you feel. There is no one who can explain this emptiness that you feel within, this boredom with how you live, this dreariness that promises you nothing but more juvenile entertainment on the screen. I am here for all of you, when your relationships break down, when you cannot stand the sight of your spouse, when your children are driving you mad with their demands, when your boss keeps screaming at you for no good reason, I am here – and I see what is happening both within your life and within your being, and within your earth.

This is why I come now, this is why I am here – not to threaten you with the possibility of the destruction of your earth, not to shake you to your core with fear and punishment and threats, I am here with love in my heart and being, I am here to show you that all of you have many spiritual guides and protectors watching over you –

who will show you ways to move beyond your current difficulties, with simple easy techniques that even children could learn. We cannot wave a magic wand, you would not want your free will taken away, we cannot solve all your problems for you, but certainly we can show you how to cope better with them yourself and how to manage them more effectively in the future. We are not spiritualists, we are humanists, life-ists, we are pro evolution, pro rectifiers, we seek your release from your self-imposed prison – we have the key to your freedom – you simply need to learn how to put the key in the lock and how to turn it in the right direction for your release. Have no fear beloveds with us much is possible, while you continue to doubt and undermine our existence and care are you doomed to live a mechanical life filled with doubt, difficulty and pain. Hear me, hear my words and know absolutely beyond any doubt if you can trust in me and my words are you safeguarding yourself and your future. My invisibility is pertinent, as you need to learn trust and a real impermeable faith – anyone can follow blindly a miracle worker in the flesh, but not everyone can trust in this sense within them that knows this is the truth even if the guru is only being channelled onto the page. Go within and feel your reaction to my words, this is where your faith and trust will stem.

If you want to move forward from where you are this is most definitely your opportunity – you do not have to necessarily go along with the status quo which appears curious about everything but which attempts or trusts nothing. Here is your door to real experience, why not indulge it for a while.

Of course it is going to be difficult at first to learn ways of moving beyond the everyday, for you like the everyday, you have grown accustomed to your everyday trivialities. You like watching the latest from you tube, you like being messaged all the time, you like being busy with work, you like interacting with friends and family. This busy lifestyle is what you have chosen so of course you must enjoy it. Rather this than getting bored I am sure you would respond. Boredom, sitting, just being with yourself is certainly the curse of your era – no one likes just being anymore, now you have to become.

Yet it is this fear of boredom which must then be held accountable for your unwillingness to go within and it is your unwillingness to go within which is directly impacting all of your relationships and sense of being loved. If you could see clearly how your fear of boredom, of being alone guides your path in an outwards direction away from love, you may be able to redeem yourself you may be able to understand what I am attempting to convey to you. But, as going outwards all the time is your way of life, and you see nothing wrong with it, this will be much more difficult for you.

Just as accepting that you are denying your feelings everyday moment by moment will be difficult for you to grasp – so too is your avoidance of boredom hazy and unclear. The question you then have to ask yourself is: 'How long can you continue like this without suffering consequences as a result?' How long will it be until this sense of loneliness although you live with others elopes and devours you? How long will it be before you recognise that the life you are currently leading is going downhill, how long before your health deteriorates, your income declines, your relationships pull the stuffing out of you? How long can you simply distract yourself from your problems by going to the pub, watching TV, going online, gambling, shopping, chasing women, chasing men, chasing children, chasing what you don't have. How long before you see the price that you are secretly paying for this blatant denial of your feelings?

How absurd is your addiction to denial? And how much more absurd it looks when it can easily be rectified by taking a few moments each day just to see your feelings. If you were to write down on one side of the page all the things you have to do to avoid feeling your emotions and then write down on the other side of the page what you would have to do to see them, and how much time each activity took, certainly the page would be so lopsided that you would have to go over the page just for one side. I am here to show you what you do not want to look at. What is the point in me expending so much energy and time to create this book if I were only going to amuse you, distract you like all your other pursuits? If I actually wasn't going to show you anything new, anything worthwhile, anything that will make a real difference in your life. I am so in tune with all of you, I am so aware of all of your hang ups, that I know I have to make a stand, argue with you just to get you to want to take a peek at what I am going to elaborate lengths to explain. For you people of earth just want to stick your head in the sand over and over again. Buddha and Jesus could right at this moment be on earth in the body riding with you on your trains, buses and planes, he could work right next to you in your office, at your school, your church or temple, he could be your next door neighbour but you people just wouldn't recognise him for all you can see is sand.

You may believe that you are an intelligent, aware, compassionate species, but I think that even this is a stretch for you to actually come at. I think you know how much trouble you are in. I think late at night when you are sitting up watching the late shows, or surfing the net cause you cannot sleep. I think you know that there is more to this picture, I think you know how terrible a place you are all in, just because you feel so terrible, restless, angry, frustrated, confused, and unsure late at night. You do not admit this, instead you worry about what will happen at work, what will happen to the kids, you direct your concerns and awareness of things not being right onto smaller frames, smaller boxes, things that you can handle, things that you can grasp. It is easier to contemplate how you will help your kids create better lives, rather than just feeling the dread, the fear, the uncertainty that exists within you, and your life. This is how you cope, you compartmentalise, you reduce things down to a form that you think you can deal with. But at the end of the day you cannot deal with anything, you cannot control what does or does not happen within your life, and within your family. You have absolutely no control, but rather than admit this you reduce things into smaller parts, things you can work with, things that make you feel more powerful and in control. An asteroid could come tomorrow and wipe all of you out – you know this, but how often do you seriously contemplate it? Why are you not preparing for this possibility? You simply cannot prepare for this - you are nothing more than parasites on a planet that could at any moment extinguish you. The awareness of this is overwhelming and terrifying – but until you can see and acknowledge how little control you actually do have over your life, you will continue to reduce it into smaller parts which greatly distort your place in the grander scheme of things.

Only when you can acknowledge how little control you actually do have will you be able to admit and understand that listening to me and my words is or may not be such a bad idea. Only when you can see outside the blinders that you have all deliberately imposed upon yourselves so that you can maintain this illusion of control, will you be able to get back on track and interact within life in the way that you were intended to. A way that refreshes you, invigorates you, restores you, and enlivens you. I am not speaking a myth or fairy-tale, I am speaking the truth – if you were to live in a fashion more aligned to the earth, to your plane of existence, you would naturally tune into and be aligned with the naturally occurring gifts and premises of this reality. These gifts offer you greater energy, a bigger perspective and understanding of life, of the cosmos, greater clarity of mind, greater ability to intuitively know what is the right decision, without the current resistance, confusion, frustration and paranoia that you live with.

Even if this theory could only offer you this, surely it is worth taking your head out of the sand just for a moment to see?

This in the end is what you must do if you are to avoid catastrophe within your life. You may think that you are the victim of a savage universe that indiscriminately hurls rocks into your life to test you see what you are made of, but unfortunately for you the obstacles within your life arise because you simply are not aware of what is happening on the many layers and levels within you. You are all multidimensional beings – you all have a multitude of forces living within you and around you at any given moment each pulling and tugging with the others to see who will win.

Just as earth is conflicted by humanities presence so too are you conflicted by these energies that are housed within you. All your atoms reduce to mostly empty space, which carries light, energy, and when you observe energy scientists can detect many levels of frequency and vibration. The frequency or pitch for any given level i.e. infra-red waves, microwave waves, radio waves, your thoughts also have their own plane and all these various types of waves, energies and vibrations interact within you, and around you moment to moment.

The light quotient in your heart at any given moment might change which then either speeds up your heart rate, or slows it down, your heart may even miss a beat. Energy is constantly pouring into you from everywhere, these energies within your heart, may be the polar opposite to those within your mind, within your cells, within your muscles, organs, brain, neurons, synapses. Your system is constantly attempting to cope with these energies, and they formulate your thoughts, your feelings, your aches and pains, your hormone levels, your energy levels, everything.

You cannot possibly be aware of all this, but regardless it goes on without your awareness for the main part and is the foundation on which everything within your life occurs. If you allow a certain vibration into your being, it may conflict with another frequency already within you – this conflict may cause heartburn, indigestion, and this process may zap energy from you making you feel tired worn out and lethargic, this tiredness may change the thoughts within your mind, so that you start to think negative thoughts such as you are not good enough, you are unlovable, nobody loves you, you are worthless, you are ugly, fat etc.

These feelings and thoughts then may make you more sensitive to what others say, you may become moody, aggressive, depressed, and anxious all because you have refused to look at the root of the problem and take the bull by the horns. If you remain within these negative states for a time your wife who may already be within her negative states may just all of a sudden say 'enough is enough 'and leave, or you may have a fight leading into a form of domestic violence, your fighting may upset one of your children that much that they start taking drugs, overdose, or decide to leave school.

Everything ripples out, absolutely everything. You cannot afford to leave these thoughts, feelings, emotions and energies unchecked, you must seek to gain control of them rather than allowing them to move you like a pawn on a chess board. If you cannot you will pay a very high price for your denial, you will pay a severe cost. Even if your wife does not leave, she will just remain pissed with you – even if you do not have a tremendous row you will still hold resentments against each other, slowly closing each of you down more so to each other, life, goodness and positive opportunities and possibilities. Even if your child does not start taking drugs, or go out onto the streets because they can't stand the fighting or the tension anymore, or leave school it may come through another avenue they may be bullied at school or they may start bullying others, their grades may slip, they may lose interest, they may start to hang out with the wrong crowd. All these things are possible because the energy you are housing remains within you, emanating outwards from you and affecting immediately those in your environment. While you still hold onto the seed of that energy, it like a beacon in the night lights up and affects and influences all within its range. When it then meets another beacon emanating from another family member much tension and conflict may result. You may say the conflict comes back to the child not listening to you, your wife not understanding your viewpoint, but all this can and is reduced to energy.

If you can resolve the energy crisis, if you can free and release the energy within you then it will not appear as obvious to you that your children are not listening to you, it will not seem as if your wife just does not understand, for once that energy is gone it can no longer facilitate the thoughts within you about these circumstances. This is where the root of the problem lies, this is where you need to pay attention within your life, this is how you make a difference within your life – everything else that you may do will be undone in time if the energy housed within you remains.

This is why I have come – to set you free, to help you to see what lies within you and to make it a more convenient and comforting activity so that it does not appear so weird or out there. This is how you cure yourself , this is how you safeguard yourself, this is how you breakthrough denial, you pay attention to what is within you, you pay attention to the thoughts feelings and energies housed within you. This gives you a feeling of freshness, this gives you a feeling of aliveness, connectedness alertness and lightness which currently is foreign to you. But this does not mean it is impossible, or fictitious, it just means you haven't experienced it yet.

Using the tune in exercise each day helps you to clear the lower planes or levels within your being, opening you up to greater spiritual experience and ability to digest and absorb the energies that you find within these experiences. The more you can accept readily the vibrations from these spiritual experiences the more spiritual experiences you will have, and the more concrete will be their affect. If you do not clear your lower levels of being you may have spiritual experiences but will be unable to harness them in real life, and put them to good use.

In other words your children will still anger and frustrate you, your husband will still annoy you, your boss will still be demanding and conceited and you will have to work through the energy that you pick up from these emotions and experiences day after day. If you do not these energies and psychological difficulties from everyday life, will overwhelm you forcing you to run to leave to get away from the source of difficulty. This means that rather than embracing and being receptive to life and those around you, you avoid them, neglect them and this will and must close you down once again to life and living, experience and energy. Once this begins happening you will lose the ability to have spiritual experience you will have to make do with much less and you will have to suffice with the scraps that your closed being allows you to glimpse at.

This then creates room for the energies within you to devour you, forcing you to close yourself down extensively so that you are like a steel cylinder nothing getting in or out, no growth, just this hard cold steel like shell that is empty within. You may still have the ability of your mind, you may be quite adept at wielding spiritual philosophy but the energy will not emanate from your being as it should, as a true teacher or healer would. Is this what you really want? Of course it is not, but it will happen if you do not clear your lower layers, if you do not work on going within daily to see your reactions to life, your emotions and feelings.

This is after all not that hard, and is the key to helping you move beyond the density of earthly life. There is no retreat that you can go to that will heal or resolve this issue, you must be prepared to go within and deal with the mud of your life, the things you don't want to see, no matter how unspiritual, selfish, ugly, greedy or needy it makes you feel, you must go within and clear this mud away otherwise risk losing everything that you hope to gain through any of your current spiritual pursuits.

To assist you to really work with this idea you could choose to go and work with a hypnotherapist to discover some of the beliefs hidden within you from childhood or past lives. Or if you have heard of a good psychotherapist this may also prove to be worthwhile. I am also going to give you some other exercises here to help you to see more accurately what lies within you. But before I do you need to realise that although Jesus and Buddha appeared to be selfless and loving with no anger, greed, or hatred within them, you must see that this does not mean that they did not experience these emotions. They just saw them coming, they were so adept at looking within and recognising what lay there that they easily could see anger coming from a far off distant place, as they watched it approach, the very fact that they had their eye on it, dissolved it immediately once it was inside their being.

Buddha's still feel the gamut of emotion like everyone else, they have to as the energies that precipitate these emotions exist upon the earth and while they exist on earth they pick up these energies like the rest of humanity. They will become gradually more attuned to higher frequencies so that lower frequencies are less and less likely to intrude, but they will still receive these energies. But they do not allow the entrance of these states such as anger, greed, hatred to unsettle them, they look at them like they would anything else, it is their overall awareness which see's everything which destabilises lower energies, and they then need do little but watch with the same gentle calm awareness that they approach everything with. It is not about the thoughts in your mind, it is not a slur to your name to notice anger, greed, lust, frustration within you, it is the awareness and the attitude that you bring to it, which will determine how these resonances impact you and your life.

Remember always that it is the seeing itself which is important, not what is looked upon. Anchor yourself into the seeing, into the witness or observer perspective with attention to not only that you are seeing and what you are seeing, but become the seeing, become the energy that see's, then all else will fade become the irrelevant nonsense that it is. This is how you transmute these types of vibration, this is how you remain open and receptive and transcend lower frequencies and energies. Never close yourself off from anything, from any thought, feeling, situation, person or perspective, instead even when 99% of your being wants to turn away – face and open to what is making you cringe, making you want to shrivel up and die, turn and face the person you dislike and just be there with them, you do not have to change or fix them, you do not have to argue with them or stand up for yourself, just be there in that space with them, allow them to be as they are and allow yourself to be as you are. This is all you can do, this is the best you can do, this will begin to transform your perception, your dislikes, your hatred fear and angst, just be with these people, just be with your emotions just be with whoever and whatever you encounter – just share the space - just be there.

If you can do this you will begin to transform your life and your being you will uncover an ancient method of practice which transforms the everyday into the sacred, it is not where you are or whom you are with, it is what you do with that that matters. If you can just be in the moment with no judgement, no attempt to resolve the issue at hand, no attempt to prove your worth or show the other person up, if you can just be with your fighting kids without having to stop them, punish them, redirect them, if you can just be there when someone is belittling you attacking you blaming you, if you can just be there with no need to do anything in return, just be there stand there, and not close down, and not judge and not attempt to flee you will begin to sense and feel that you can change the dynamics of your life, making each and every moment more sacred than when you are meditating on top of a mountain, or praying in a temple or mosque, then everything evens out, the bumps of life smooth before your eyes and all of a sudden what at one time annoyed the hell out of you has become sacred, empty, spacious, invigorating even. Offering you energy rather than taking it from you.

This creates a sense of wellbeing which is above and beyond that of the everyday this connects you to your core being, and heightens your awareness automatically – this gives you space within your mind and within your life just to be, just to relax into each moment without the jargon of having to please, having to impress. This frees you from the resonances within you that would pull you back down into selfish need, demands and moods which have you swinging like a pendulum from one extreme to the other. This creates highs and lows within all your emotional states and creates an imbalance that can lead to mental disorders such a bi polar, depression, anxiety and self-hatred. These disorders are treated with medications more and more, leaving you with no real resolution or cure. Even if you then go into meditation you will find the freedom you receive from this to be short lived, temporary and disconnected from who you are and where you are in life.

Remaining open to each moment, to every situation, to every person you encounter is an authentic practice which opens you up to this spaciousness which is my definition of love – when you practice this each day – when you remind yourself to be open each morning, when you tell yourself just to be receptive when you get out of the car and walk into work, when you remind yourself again at morning tea break, when you start to just be with the whingers and complainers at work, and rather than join in with their whinging you just hear them and be with them and understand them, and stay in this spaciousness which exists within you and within each moment, you nourish understanding, love, gentleness, openness and unity.

Love then is not a note like money which you believe you have given to others, it is not something you give to them out of the goodness of your heart to remind them of later – it is alternatively the ability just to step back into this spaciousness that surrounds you, and fills you within each moment. Just to be in that moment, even if you cannot feel the spaciousness yet, it will come, it will come. Just be in that moment, to not rehearse what you are going to say or how you are going to respond, just focus on just being there in the moment and whatever comes up and out of your mouth comes. Do not censor or adjust what you say, just allow whatever comes no matter how seemingly irrelevant, stupid, cold or plain it appears to be just to come. You do not have to heal anyone, you do not have to console or comfort or fix, just be there in the moment, just allow yourself to be in this space which will nourish you and will also without your awareness nourish others.

This is the best and the only path to take if you desire to free yourself from your anguish, pain, burden and regret. Just practicing this when you are with people, as often as you remember, not concerned if you forget, just being in the moment even if you are alone, just sinking beneath the surface into the centre of your being and watching and greeting the scorn that you have for yourself for not remembering with gentleness and an undisturbed being will lift you up and above the everyday to a place which is sacred.

This is not about constantly imposing the idea upon yourself that you need to be in the moment, in the here and now – it is not a practice of mindfulness where you continually feel like you need to focus on your movements rather than get caught up in your thoughts. This is the opposite of this practice – this practice greets thoughts no matter how confusing or jumbled or irrelevant with the love and appreciation of the gentle being which exists behind all and everything, your awareness. No matter what you encounter, no matter how remiss you have been you simply greet whatever is there in the moment with a gentle acceptance and appreciation. No matter what you find you greet it with openness and care, you do not allow your being or mind to become upset disturbed by the thought, the action the behaviour, you simply open even to this and allow this to be there seen as part of the source of goodness which created you and is you.

Nothing is outside of you, nothing is evil, nothing is good and nothing is bad, there is no truth and no deception, there is no yin and yang, not dark and light, no success and failure, no right and wrong, all is part of the same energy the energy of creation and you simply greet whatever you find with the love and the care that you would greet a beloved friend or honoured guest. You open and trust and welcome this into your being – thoughts are no enemies, they are part and parcel of creation, offering you energy and resonance at each moment. Open to them, bring a calm awareness to them and you will begin to feel the beauty and majesty contained within them and within everything which has been created within this life and domain.

This is how you cure yourself and your life and even your thoughts, this is how you begin to be able to stop judging, categorising and alienating people, thoughts, things, and emotions. No emotion is not worthy of god, no feeling is sinful, evil or unacceptable, all simply is energy, is life, is force, and these forces must be part and parcel of the energies that created you and sustain you and this life, this world, the air you breathe, the trees that clean the air. All and everything is God is Jesus, is Buddha is creation – even the desire to sleep with your friends husband, the desire to win lotto, the desire to earn more money, beat someone else in a race, or a job promotion, to have better behaved kids than your friends, to have smarter kids than your friends, to be better dressed, have a bigger house, to go on more holidays all these thoughts are manifestations of the creative energy of life, and should be greeted with calm awareness and kindness, openness, receptivity.

If you can work towards this, if you can at least spend a few days experimenting with it, you will find that this approach to life has an enormous impact on your relationships, your sense of feeling loved and connected, and the problems that you encounter. You will if you persevere with this mind set begin to see your difficulties and problems dissolving right in front of your nose without you having to do anything. Because this space that you sink into within each moment, this kindness and receptivity that you greet each person with is the creative force of life – it is the potent energy that has created all and everything that you encounter within this realm.

Like a lake or a pond of energy silently existing within you, the more you dip yourself into it, even if just for a moment or two, within the situations or quiet moments within your lives, the more you are connected to and with the life force, the heightened plane of awareness which simply is. This then helps to smooth the road of creation out in front of you, it undoes the trouble that your ego or personality will naturally get you into. When you can step back from your personality and its need to be involved and to fix everything, when you stand back and sink silently, and quietly into this pond of energy within you, even while speaking with or listening to a friend or co-worker, or while sitting up alone at night, you re energise yourself and your being and your life. Like plugging yourself back into an energy circuit you invigorate and refresh your life. Like restarting a stubborn machine that won't work properly plugging back in to this inner pond, clears vibrations within you which may be fuelling your difficulties and desires. By dipping into this pond of aware stillness, openness and receptivity that accepts everything as god or life, you refresh and clear and reset your being, your day or each moment, so that something totally different and new can be born and sustained.

This is how you overcome your denial, this is how you begin to open to what is within you in an honest, meaningful way. Other techniques have their pros and cons, this one has a rate of effectiveness which is second to none. To assist you with this idea more fully I will offer you now a visualisation meditation that you can work with to accentuate and develop this inner pond, or lake. If you work with this meditation it will be easier for you to remember to dip back into it within everyday life, when you are driving your car, when you are speaking or listening to a friend, when you are on the computer, when you are watching TV, when you are walking or exercising.

Inner Pond Reflection

Sit quietly for a few moments just watching the world – then close your eyes, and count backwards from 10 to 0 slowly feeling as if you are sinking back into yourself more so with each number.

Then relax as you enter your inner realm – take a few moments just to notice how you feel here and get comfortable with the surrounds, the sensations, the noise, and the colours.

Now within this space picture a brilliantly shining pond or lake that exists right in the middle of your being. This lake is luminous, it shines as if sun is reflecting off the water. It appears to have some ethereal glow, some magnetic force to it. Just look at this magnificent lake, and take it in, enjoy its tranquillity and beauty.

Now see yourself beside the lake, and you slowly then walk into the lake and have a swim, a gentle warm, wonderful swim. The water is not cold, it is heated, temperate and warm. Feel yourself immersing into this lake which is more energetic than watery, and enjoy swimming within it.

Feel it invigorating you, soothing you, replenishing you. Bask and swim within it for as long as you like. Then as you leave the lake sense and feel yourself being totally refreshed and alive, like warm wind blowing on the water still on your skin, you awaken and feel more in tune more connected to where you are.

Know that when you return from this place, that somehow something is different.

What is Love? Messages from Mary on Love and Fulfilment

Maya

Chapter Six – Unravelling Love.

Beloved Ones I am Mary,

I come forward at this time to reassure you that you are moving toward something - a larger perspective – you are not just running around chasing your tails. From our vantage point certainly it seems at times as if all of you are chasing your tails, but you will move away from this as time wears on and you see the futility of your current actions. All of you have simply become content with discontent, and it is far better to live with the devil you know than the one you don't.

Thus, I need to literally argue with you to help you see above and beyond your current scope of reality. I need you to become aware that indeed there is more to this life than what you currently perceive. The best way for me to do this is to help you see how dysfunctional and grotesque one of your pillars has become, and the pillar I have chosen is love. The love that you have created on earth is in truth not that enviable, if it were in a better condition undoubtedly you as a species would not be in the predicament you are currently within. The fact that so many of you feel unloved and unlovable and unworthy is a direct consequence of the love that you have bought and sold.

Love to you has become little more than a means of getting you what you want, love is not the platform on which you live your life, love has become something rare and precious that you offer to only the most worthy of beings within your hierarchy of friends and companions. To deserve your love these people have to show kindness to you first, if they do not then they shall not receive your love. Only the good are loved, only the righteous, only the saintly, the do gooders, the ones who follow laws, morals ethics. All else are judged unlovable, detestable even and this is why you have so many prisons, this is why you have huge immigration centres all overflowing to capacity.

From the outside this perspective of love may appear fair enough, everyone has to follow laws, has to participate, has to conform and help sustain the type of society that you have created and bought into. It is of course unbeneficial to let rebel rousers, trouble makers and aggressors get away with violent acts or selfish disregard for others. Yet, the punishment and banishment that you now impose on such members of your society only perpetuates and breeds a level of dissent which can only multiply and grow.

Rather than addressing this obvious fact you have instead once again stuck your head in the sand not wanting to deal with such obvious facts, and then let your governments deal with such waywards – for as long as you do not need to encounter them you can acquiesce the methodology somewhat. But my dear ones, the only way for you to transform your society is from the bottom up – if you want change if you want a better more evolved, less aggressive and violent, and narrow minded society you have to address the way in which you treat those who have wronged.

This is not to say that you need be soft and limp and syrupy, love is not weak, it is the strongest force that you can know, it's just your misinterpretations have left you without viable evidence of its strength. Perhaps this is why you have so easily abandoned it within your daily life, as its obvious broadness and depth has come across to you as wishy washy, lax and without any real potency. Yet, this is and can be only a misperception on your part. Gravity is the weakest force in the universe and yet look at what it sustains. Look at its impact within your world and others. Without gravity you could not exist, without gravity are you lost in a wasteland of continual chaotic movement and space.

Love like gravity appears invisible at first, yet once you see its effect on objects and people you can have a much better understanding of its potency and power. Love is not just a feeling that you have when your child is born, or when you meet the love of your life – love is not just a good deed that you pull out of your hat for someone worthy – love is not something you do to earn merit points, to be seen as saintly, to get into heaven, to create a good name – love also is not only a state of awareness within your mind – love is the essential ingredient within all and everything.

Love exists within you and us, and is all of us, love is the momentum that created this world, it is an energetic force that enables everything that exists to exist. Love is a certain vibratory rate that facilitates higher and higher ascension and broadness of perception. Love is the energy that fuels your physical body, your mental body your spiritual body. Love exists whether you are aware of it or not, love exists alongside everything that you do and don't do, love perpetuates feelings of wholeness and care, and it also perpetuates feelings of hate and discord.

Love is the basis of life, love is all around you all the time regardless of whether you live alone, or are surrounded by a multitude of family and friends. Love exists, and love is – there is nothing you can do to deserve or warrant or earn it – you are already it, and it is you. You are already within the kingdom of heaven, there is no rapture of ascension into heaven to look forward to, you are already here. God is here, love is here, tenderness and joy and bliss and ecstasy are right here now, they are within you as you reading this – they sit beside you and in front of you at work. It walks past you in the street, you see it in the sky in the trees in the rivers, rocks, insects and birds – love is here, love is now, love is constant, it does not change just because your emotions do – love is within and beyond emotion, love is above your mind, within your mind, and below your mind. Love just is – whether you choose to acknowledge this or not is your choice, and love does not even care if you do not acknowledge it, for love does not need you to approve, to see to be aware, to become enlightened, realised, in tune with it or nature or everything. Love is everywhere, it is everything, it does not need your awareness to be so, it does not need your acceptance or approval to continue to do what it has been doing all along. Love is energetic substance which sustains us, you and me, and everything else within the universe.

This is why everyone is cared for whether they know it or not, this is why no matter what happens everything always turns out alright, this is why good things happen and why not so good things happen – love intermixes with and sustains them all – when you are downtrodden and depressed and uncertain you feel something within in certain moments you feel almost another force within or beside you. You feel amongst the shame and meaninglessness, numbness and or emotion another force somewhere within you, pulling you through, getting you up in the morning making you feel better after a night where you could not see past this sense of overwhelming meaninglessness and torture.

You feel love when you have been busy and you are exhausted then all of a sudden you stop, you rest, you are forced to not do anything, you feel it within you then, you feel a force inside you grounding you into your being, into your life, getting you through, somehow pulling you to the other side of what needs to be done. Although you don't think you can go on, you are tired and out of sorts and upset burdened, yet there is this force pulling you onwards, this is love. When people get caught in inconceivable circumstances, they are out at sea and all of a sudden a storm swells up and they are caught right in the middle, the waves surge, the rain is pelting down, the boat is rocking and tipping and letting in water, the clouds are black, they batten down and do what they can and prepare for the worst, and their boat may tip, they may end up in the water, but eventually the sun comes out. Through it all, when they feared the worst they felt this force that somehow got them through, and knew they would be ok. They do not know what this force is, they do not know it by name so they cannot refer to it, describe it, recall it and so they dismiss it. But this is love – love is always there it has to be, it has no choice, it is the energy of life, it is everything.

What is Love? Messages from Mary on Love and Fulfilment

When everything that appears to be dissolves, still there will be love – love is the stuff of life, the substance of the immaterial as well as the material. Love is always there beside and within you, on the footy oval when you need to outrun an opponent to get closer to the mark or the goal, love is there on the dance floor when you have had a few drinks and you really begin to let your hair down and feel alive and are having fun. Love is there when you are saying goodnight to your child, love is between you and within each of you, love is there when you are arguing with your spouse, when you feel like they are not listening to you or respecting you, love is there inside you seeking to be seen, seeking connection, union oneness love is there pulling you toward each other when you want the fight to be over, and love is there pushing you apart when you want your own space and freedom from the treachery of misunderstanding.

Love is there constantly within your lives, and it is unconcerned if you are aware of it or not, for you are in it, and of it, you cannot be outside of it – love like the prodigal son's father just waits patiently. Love is unconcerned that people are building bombs and planning attacks, love is unconcerned that people are killing each other, attacking each other, abusing each other, love is not bothered by the gangs that are plotting against each other, that are distributing large masses of drugs to the younger generations, love is unmoved by the dictators who take money from their people to buy weapons and niceties for their girlfriends and wives. Love is unswayed when a man rapes a child, love is unchanged when a child kills that man many years later. Love just is. Love is buoyant it remains constant regardless of form or feature.

When you can as an individual recognise this precept, when you can acknowledge the continuous flow of what is, regardless of form or shape or colour, texture or temperature, you can begin to unravel yourself so that you flow with this current rather than oppose it. This does not mean going with the flow, it does however mean recognising a higher good, a greater awareness within all and everything. This is the appeal of all of your religions, and theosophy, this is what makes it a universal drawcard as people like to think that there is a higher power watching over them, caring for them, sustaining them, for when their own prowess and power run thin, it is good to know you have someone else on your team.

This is what religion is making a bargain with life – I will be good and do as you ask if and only if you let me through the gates of heaven. If God were to somehow materialise and tell all his people across the earth that indeed there is no heaven, and that after life on earth only hell exists how long would all his people be able to keep being good? Surely the temptation to be bad, to let morals slide would increase? Surely people would want more fun in their life, and fun comes from doing things you are not meant to do. Why did Adam and Eve eat the forbidden apple, because it was fun that's why – because it made them feel free and alive and liberated.

If God does exist, he is love, for this is the energy of the universe, and if he is love this overrides all else – nothing else matters, love will still stand at the end. If this could be so, there is no heaven and hell there can only be love – if there is only love with no heaven or hell then the guides set forth by Jesus can only be to show you how to see and recognise this love. It can only be a method to open you up to this love, so that you can bear witness to it in the everyday.

If this is so, this would greatly revolutionise the way in which the bible is read, and I would guess that people would actually find greater meaning and purpose within it. If turning the other cheek, if loving your brother like Jesus loved you opens you up to a real authentic love now within the everyday then its merit is more rewarding and restoring. Then the passages of the bible contain more relevant information – for even the best Christians become uncertain not only if they will get into heaven but if there is a heaven at all before they die. This makes their death laborious and difficult this makes their death a chore, something to be feared and ran from rather than something to embrace and welcome.

You would think after living on earth for so long seeing the immense changes of the earth seeing the chaos and the confusion and the difficulty of living on earth that people would embrace and look forward to it – but sadly this is not the case – people do ridiculous things just to avoid death, and although they cannot move perhaps, and are bedridden, still they lay there refusing to give in, refusing to go as the fear of what may lay ahead is so terrifying that it overcomes them and all their senses.

If Christianity, Hinduism, Buddhism or Islam could create results for their devotees within this life then I think the overall message and methodology of religion could be improved and have greater effect and result in devotee's lives. Delaying rewards until the afterlife almost punishes the disciple now in this life, as if they are evil, as if they are of original sin, as if no matter what they do they are condemned to tyranny and enslavement, there is no freedom, no path away from the curse of being on earth – only by doing good works, only by becoming like an angel then do you then have hope that you may see what heaven looks like. It also puts undue pressure on the afterlife, and makes you all frightened of it, for fear that things are different to what you believe. This fear of death is even more devastating in its consequence than postponing the reward of good works.

This fear of the afterlife has you all denying anything that may give you clues to it – ghosts and spirits are denied for somehow their presence negates the image of heaven, and this terrifies you all tremendously. Not only do you need to then deny anything that may contradict your perception of heaven, you are all obsessed with becoming younger, with living longer, with doing as much as you can in this life, hoping to some extent that it will be enough to prove your worth to those angels on high who are the gatekeepers to heaven.

These two negative consequences of your postponement of joy til the afterlife are the seeds that have crippled your society and its possibilities. If you could change your religious perceptions to make the rewards of heaven available now two very grand things would happen on earth. People would feel free to experience joy now, totally and absolutely with no shame or fear or condemnation, and from this would heightened natural spiritual experiences flow – which will give you naturally a greater sense of connection to love, to the universe and to each other, and this would reduce relationship conflict and consequence, and many of the dysfunctions you have as a result of guilt, shame, unworthiness, self-hatred. Another wonderful thing would also occur – you would cease to be frightened of death – if you can experience joy now in each day, in your own way without anyone looking over your shoulder shaking their head or telling you what a fool you made of yourself, how outrageous was your behaviour, if you could be free to experience joy now, your personal inhibitions would also dissolve. When you allow yourself the freedom to move beyond your beliefs, conditioning and inhibitions, you enter the spaciousness of life that surrounds you, is within you, and when you are in this space there is no fear, you are aligned to your core – you are an overflowing of joy and gratitude, happiness, peace and content. Then there is no doubt, absolutely no doubt that death can only contain in essence what you have found at the core of your being. This awareness, this knowing, this honest and unashamed truth of being easily and naturally transcends all. This is Love, this is my dear ones what you are looking for – this is the only cure, the only solution to the puzzle of your life and way of life.

The solutions that you have found to relieve your heartache, your loneliness, your disappointment, your fear and mistrust, your pain and your guilt are not really solutions they in truth only cover over the gap for a time. They soothe you for a time that is it, they do not fix or heal anything, and at some point you must return to the awareness that indeed your life still is haunted by these aspects, continually. Love is the cure, love is the path, all the philosophy that you have heard and read is indeed accurate and true. You just don't know how to find and capture this love, you cannot find it or even if you do you cannot sustain it indefinitely.

If love is to be real and effective within your lives it must be ongoing, it must be permanent. That is why you have failed to recognise to date how ineffective your version of love is as you accept that it may be absent for large periods of time. You rarely even expect it to visit you now as marriage and responsibility appear to have taken control. Now that you can get married you could almost completely avoid love or feeling love totally and still live a normal everyday life where you think that you are doing everything that you are meant to be doing and experiencing everything that you are meant to be experiencing. When in truth you are not, you are limited and disabled and cut off from one of the most important experiences of being on earth – love.

Marriage gives you a set of rules, honour maybe not obey, be there in sickness and in health, respect, etc. All you now have to do is perform within this role, provide for your family be there at dinner time, and sometimes not even this, but basically just show up and you have the epitome of what all people on earth esteem. Regardless of how you feel about this, regardless of how happy or unhappy you are, regardless of the feelings and ideas and yearnings that you need to suppress to manage it, marriage makes you a bona fide love basket.

Then years down the track you stare out the window and wonder what happened to your life? Why are you not happy? You have done everything that you were meant to, you met a nice girl, you have romantic dinners out, even if you drink too much and end up fighting on the way home in the car, you do everything that you are supposed to and still there is something missing, still if you had to exactly pin point what love is you would struggle. Yet, you continue to accept that this is the way it is meant to be, that there is nothing else, that there is nothing different.

The reason that you settle for so little must be because you have accepted the old religious idea that you are full of sin. Somewhere in your consciousness you have accepted the idea that you are unworthy – you may have digested this idea from a parent, an experience at church when you were very little, from a neighbour, a teacher, a cousin, there are a million and one places that you may have come across this idea and it for some reason just stuck. It stuck because this is the same belief all of you hold, so it is supported within your environment. For sure if your environment did not support this belief it would be less likely that you would have adopted it. But, as it does you then have to accept it as your own. You have no choice it just happens without your awareness, as the vibrations that exist on your plane of existence that all of you have agreed to facilitate reflect this belief that you are unworthy.

Only amongst shame is the human population happy – without guilt, shame and unworthiness you as a species it appears would not know how to exist. You have this grain embedded within your psyche, within your environment, with every brick that builds your houses and churches with every road you lay with every tree you plant. This is your status quo, shame, guilt and unworthiness are your staple diet. When you eat your food no matter how lavish, how exotic you are eating shame and guilt. This is what you have become, this is how you manage not to be aware that you do not have in love in your life, as guilt and shame are all you know they fill the void, they may not be nice or comfortable but they are the vibration that all of you have accepted as necessary for earth.

Only when you see you have the power to change this vibratory field will you be able to truly relinquish shame and guilt. And my dear ones you need to change it soon otherwise you risk the vibration of guilt and shame becoming so thick and layered upon the earth that it may become impossible for you to ever change it. If you allow this to occur, if you refuse to accept higher vibrations into your aura and field of reference, love will undoubtedly become little more than a myth. Future generations will ask their grandparents 'tell us about love grandma, what was it like.'

Love is everything – it is constant, it is within and a part and behind all, but you have severed yourself from it, and each day you are creating bigger and bigger gaps between it and you, for you are literally layering yourself in guilt and shame. Like wrapping a scarf of self-loathing around yourself to protect you from the elements, from love, are you slowly inch by inch losing contact with this love. Others will tell you that you are moving towards it in a bid to motivate you to want to be part of it, but in actual truth you as a species are segregating yourself away and apart from love.

On some level you are aware of this, ancient mythology will always describe the battles between the forces of light and dark, and at the end of the day these industrious forces reduce to love, both of them, it cannot be any other way – but certainly as you have free will, you can choose that shame and guilt become your vestiges of hope and security, and if you are to choose this you must accept the inevitable consequences that follow. Believing only in self-hatred is not a wise choice – but as you are so accustomed to not looking at anything squarely in the face, you cannot see that the beautiful woman all dressed up nice in front of you is a man. You must learn to look a little closer, you must be a touch smarter, you must see that every choice you make is a choice between love or its opposite.

There is no reason once you are aware of this choice why you should not choose love, there is no reason why you cannot choose love, and have it with you day in day out. It will and can be there 24/7 for you, you can access it at will, for it follows you, is within everything you encounter and most importantly is you. This is what the Indian gurus have been doing in their caves, this is what the mystics and the poets have been alluding to all this time, it can be with you and surround you even when you are amongst crisis, confusion, exhaustion and disease. Love like a bubble of light with the fresh air of a mountain spring follows and surrounds you always, you just need to learn ways of seeing it, feeling it, bringing into the forefront of your life and being, and this can be done even within the modern world, even amongst all the atrocity, war, disease, famine, poverty and corruption it can be done. Nothing is impossible with me at your side, nothing is out of the question, if you truly want something, if you truly yearn for it, seek it and need it, there is absolutely no question, it can become your reality.

Currently it may appear as if this concept is as far away from you as Pluto or the sun, but I assure you it can become your reality. You have free will, and that free will is potent, very potent, do not underestimate its potency. The choice to open to higher vibrations is one you will make at some point perhaps not in this life but certainly in others for this is why you exist at all to explore and expand all fields of reference not just one.

To overcome your addiction to worthlessness you need to be able to want to change your mind, your perception on life, you will need to take action and explore things that currently you have pushed aside as airy fairy or fantasy. Yet, you still watch your movies which are full of fantasy, you still daydream about things that are never going to happen in your life, you still read books that take you to faraway places, places you will never know, you can sit on a therapists couch and talk about your issues, you can see a life coach to train you in the art of manifesting anything you desire, but the simple idea of going within your own being and looking for your own soul is somehow more absurdically fantastical than all of these.

Going within your own being is the only way you will be able to relinquish your unworthiness, and only when you can however briefly let go of this can you ever hope to obtain any sort of happiness or sense of being loved and valued. While what lies within you remains unchanged anything that you do on the outer to gain love and value and happiness can at best be temporary or illusory. While you continue to trim the leaves rather than dig for and cut the root are you left to a wasteland of forces that can rise up at any moment from within you and cause you the utmost havoc and upheaval. If this is the way you choose to live and love I can do little more than stand by and watch, but don't expect God, the Universe, or someone else to bail you out when things go topsy turvy for you, for you yourself are the one who has chosen this, you yourself must get yourself out.

If you cannot see the correlation between the unworthiness that you hold within and what is happening in your life, then we are in trouble, you are destined to carry on as you are indefinitely. Only when you begin to explore this possibility and discover its reality do we have any hope. Freeing yourself involves doing things that normally you wouldn't consider, it involves going outside the parameters that your mind is comfortable within, how you think you will ever change while remaining inside the parameters of your mind is beyond me. Freedom requires immense effort, discipline and lateral thinking, you cannot just use the tools you currently depend upon for they are not working, you must either improve the tools or replace them with something more efficient.

Unworthiness is the obstruction to love, and to feeling loved, to create a greater feeling of love in your life you must be prepared to love yourself first, free yourself from the enslavement to unworthiness and self-hatred, self-criticism and scorn. Stop belittling yourself, and thinking the worst, stop self sabotaging yourself and punishing yourself. Start to ease up on yourself and feel and know that there is much for you to gain from this, much for you to appreciate and understand. If you can walk with me with this, if you can work sincerely with the exercises you find here, you will see that they do and will make a difference, the difference between feeling loved and cared for and feeling out of the loop, betrayed and uncertain all the time. Whether you admit these feelings to yourself or not they are there, and the sooner you familiarise yourself with them the better off you are going to be. Only through allowing them to be there and to be there with them will you release them from your inner world, a world where they are free to induce emotions and states of being which perpetuate much of your difficulty within this life.

I am aware of how difficult this idea is to many of you, as you would prefer to deny that even you feel this way – you like to think that you are doing ok, you like to think that things are not that bad, you like to think that things will improve. When things get better for you, when things are comfortable, then there is simply no need to go within, to feel these uncomfortable emotions, then they become irrelevant. But unfortunately for you this is not the case, they linger there creating absolute havoc for you if not now in the future – one day suddenly you get a phone call and your world is turned upside down, one day your son does not come home and your world is turned upside down, one day you are let go from work, you discover your wife is having an affair and suddenly your world turns upside down.

Yet, these thoughts, and feelings which you have repressed are the culprits for your turmoil, like termites they have been eating away at the structure of your life all this time, and then suddenly one day you discover your house is worthless, all the while they were eating under your nose, while you were eating and sleeping and watching TV, all along it was happening, you could have stopped or prevented it at any moment, but you simply were not aware, you simply did not know. That is why I am here to show you, to get you in touch with what is happening within you – to make it more appealing to you, and to make it a necessity not even a luxury.

The value of this has been greatly underestimated within your current society – in truth unless you are doing some Buddhist retreat which seems to be the done thing to do, going within your own soul is more or less taboo. The reasons for this are a little obscure if someone were to ask people generally would shrug their shoulders – for you all are unaware why you have not been shown how to go within your being. Overall it is simply easier not to, it is easier to blame and project your own emotions onto what is happening outside of you, out in front. It is not so easily to turn 180 degrees and look within.

Your unworthiness, your unlovableness, you self-hatred, your sense of being wrong, of being not good enough, of being in the way, impacts the thoughts within your mind moment to moment. These beliefs are like filters which either accept or reject a particular thought which seeks entry to your mind. The more unworthy you feel, the more you will reject thoughts of love and feeling loved, of appreciation and harmony, peace and joy. Thus although happiness has become the topic of the moment all of you are shutting it out minute by minute. Your belief that you are unworthy prohibits you from allowing it to enter, like salt on a wound love aggravates and annoys this belief that you are unworthy. It contradicts it and undermines its authority so of course it will shake its head when love begs for mercy at the entrance to your mind.

Only by correcting this misperception that you are unworthy and unlovable can you ever hope to move forward towards love. While you contain and hold onto the seeds of self persecution and loathing are you doomed to feel only the effects of this – anger, frustration, hopelessness, fear, dread, regret, shame, guilt, and a bored perspective which becomes accustomed to expecting little and rather than challenge this notion, accepts it and blunders on helplessly using addiction as the only means of relief.

My advice here then is to seek out a hypnotherapist, an alternative, compassionate, spiritually aware one who can help you dig down back into this notion of unworthiness and discover its origin for you. You do not want to go to a hypnotherapist who teaches you how to quit smoking, or lose weight, you need to go specifically to someone who specialises in past life regression and you need to be open to the idea that you have had past lives, and these lives more than likely hold the source of intent which has perpetuated this feeling of unlovableness and unworthiness. Once you have seen for yourself a particular circumstance or situation which may have evoked this unworthiness, this will open your eyes to an understanding that sees how everything in your life is connected and absolutely nothing is unnoticed or unaccounted for.

As weird or as unnecessary as going to a hypnotherapist may appear I urge you to at least contemplate seriously attending one – if you do you will be glad you did.

If this idea is too unappealing to you, I will also provide some exercises for you to help you reconnect with your unworthiness and pain. Even connecting to these stored energy reserves will help aid their release, as it provides a path for them to exit your being. So begin today to contemplate your unworthiness, ask yourself where is your unworthiness hiding, ask yourself why it may exist at all, ask yourself what ramifications this unworthiness might have within your life, you could journal the answers if you like, discuss it with a similar minded friend, or just contemplate when you are alone.

Ask yourself who in your life has made you feel unworthy and why? Ask yourself what you think unworthiness really means. Ask yourself in what ways your life may have been sculpted or guided by this unworthiness. What events or happenings may not have occurred due to this inner unworthiness – and what things may have happened due to this sense of being unlovable.

When things go wrong within your life, what thoughts run through your mind – make a list. When things go right in your life what thoughts run through your mind?

How do you feel when your friends have successes?

How do you feel when your friends have losses?

Who in your life makes you feel the most loved and why?

Who in your life makes you feel the most unloved and why?

How many times have people done nice things for you and still you felt unmoved or unloved?

When you are exhausted late at night, and everything is weighing heavily upon you what are the thoughts going through your mind?

If you did not feel unlovable or unworthy, how do you imagine your life might be different?

Do you think that if you did not have these thoughts of not being good enough that you would be able to better cope with your life?

Who has ultimate control over these thoughts?

These thoughts although they have been with you for quite some time, are not really your own, they come from the global consciousness that all of you contribute to and partake in. Understanding this is your freedom from them, and your liberation. Once you see that these thoughts are not real or accurate and are not even your own, letting them go is easy.

To really penetrate into these thoughts you need to be aware that they are there, you need to see that they do exist, for right now even you are not totally convinced, you are unsure, you are used to feeling their consequence, shame, lethargy, awkwardness, hopelessness, pessimism, shyness and inability to communicate effectively and assertively. But, as you have not faced them squarely in the face, as you are doing everything in your power to avoid seeing them, it is difficult then to grasp the true significance of my meaning.

Thus now we need to pierce through this façade and this layer of dense thick syrup which prevents you from seeing them accurately – so along with the previous questions you will need to answer the following questions which will hopefully get you thinking more about these thoughts, and working more intimately with them so that you can let them go.

Unlovableness — Questionnaire

When was the last time you were angry, or upset, annoyed or depressed?

What situation, circumstance or person contributed to this feeling within you?

Why did this situation induce these emotions? How did this situation make you feel?

Take time to really look at how you are feeling within this situation – you can even close your eyes and picture the situation again – see yourself and what is happening inside of you – what is really going on?

What are the main themes, thoughts, beliefs (not emotions) that seem to be surfacing within you, within this situation?

Do any of the above beliefs stem from a sense of unworthiness or unlovableness?

Can you see how indeed you may hold a belief that you are unlovable or not good enough?

Is it possible that rather than the situation provoking the emotion or belief, it may in truth be the other way round, the belief may be creating the situation?

How might this situation have been different if you did not hold this belief of being unworthy within you? Close your eyes and look at the situation again within your mind – with no belief of being unworthy, how are your reactions different to that in the first instance?

Dissolving this belief then, may significantly alter the way in which you respond to not only this situation but others, creating more space in your life for more effective communication and expression. Is this a possibility? If so, how would such a change impact and influence your life do you imagine?

Working with this idea, and seeking to find your unworthiness then, one can assume would be worthwhile and assist you to create a positive change in your life and your being. Do you agree?

Take time again sometime today to contemplate this idea – and then tomorrow agree to complete this questionnaire again looking at a different situation that has recently happened, and answer the questions with this situation in mind.

If you can work with and apply this questionnaire to several different situations within your life you will really have a good grasp on how letting go of or overriding this belief of unworthiness, or unlovableness can have great impact and effect within your life, and within your being, how you feel about things each day. Give it a go, and see what happens.

Unworthiness has infiltrated and taken over your psyche and life – although it is invisible to you and like the wind you only see it when it masses together and causes inconceivable destruction – it more potent than an alien species who has taken over your world is tearing you apart piece by piece. Only when you wake up to this, only when you see and acknowledge this can you rectify and change it. When you consider and contemplate the enormous effect that unlovableness has on your earth, when you consider how worthlessness prods and provokes and limits you, you will see that its impact and effect are far more devastating than earth events, erratic weather patterns and climate change.

More effective than not using coal fired power, breeding cattle, or driving cars, is unearthing your unworthiness going to help resolve many of the dire consequences that you see happening on earth. This sense of having to prove yourself, prove your worth is why politicians create conflict and seek to overthrow cultures and leaders dissimilar to them. This unlovableness is the cause of your relationship conflicts, your parental neglect, your teenage rebellion. The list just keeps going on and on, unworthiness is why you fail in life, why you need to comfort yourself with food, with drugs, with alcohol, with shopping and sex and exercise.

Never has a species been in the grip of such an unyielding, overbearing force, yet because it is invisible, because you are all isolated and separate from each other, you do not realise what is happening within you is also happening within others, and this ripples out as energy impacting your wildlife, your plant life, your environment, your global mindset, and creates destruction, violence, aggression, and ridiculous acts of murder, corruption, blame and self sabotage. Only when you can appreciate how this is affecting you within your life, and the enormous impact that it has had in the past, and will continue to have in the future, can you appreciate how it is impacting all of you on a global scale.

While you as a species continue to ignore this, ignore what is happening within you, ignore your pain and guilt and shame, and think that going to confession, doing good works, donating to charity, or creating a beautiful home is going to somehow compensate, then you are being even more misled and deceived. How far do you need to fall before you realise you are falling? How dirty do you need to get before you realise you are trapped in mud? Just because you can still see the sky and the clouds and the sun does not mean that you are not trapped, or not losing your freedom, your resourcefulness and specialness which is the inherent goodness of who you are.

Now is the time to stop all this work, all this busyness, all this social eating out and cooking, now is the time to get back to nature, get back to who you are and start looking at what is actually happening within you. You need to do more than just meditate or use relaxation strategies, you need to become pioneers and explorers of your inner world, and you need to start investigating what lies within. Now more than ever do you need an inner revolution. No guns, or bombs, or plotting to overthrow a diplomat, a leader, just remembering to go within and to seek to find the essence of who you are and overthrow anything that stops you from accomplishing this.

This is not about spirituality, this is not about becoming a saint, a monk, guru – this is not about becoming a flying yogi, a supernatural superhuman who can do other worldly things, this is about getting real about who you are and what you want from this life. This about being able to penetrate into your life more effectively and into others and situations more effectively. This is about being able to bring out your full potential, and to respect and care for this. You do not have to be a spiritual freak to want freedom from pain, and guilt and shame. You do not need to be out there on a limb with Shirley Maclaine to want freedom from unworthiness and this sense that you are not loved, this is what being human is all about, this is about accepting your humanity, and seeking to perfect it, free it from the snares and traps of your everyday life.

How long can you continue as you are? How long can the promise of more pay, a higher position, family life, or freedom from your mortgage keep you occupied and miserably content with discontent? How long are you able to keep up this façade with your friends and colleagues that you have it all together, are sailing through life, are happy and positive and carefree when late at night you feel morose, numb, heavy and overburdened with everything that must be done, and how soul stealing all of it is?

If you perceive you can hold this up, you can continue without too much drama or effort, of what consequence is it having on you, on your being, on your inner world when it is rarely let out to see the light. You are so accustomed to shoving everything under the carpet, you are so unaccustomed to going within that you do not realise how little air your inner world is actually getting. Like turning your back on a disabled child down in your basement are you unaware that his clothes are wet, he has not eaten his food, and that he has gone to the toilet where he is meant to be sleeping. You cannot use ignorance as an excuse when the time for owning up comes. When the time of death is at hand what will you tell yourself, how will you explain what you have done to your inner world, to your being, to the energetic force that created and blessed you?

Perhaps I am just ranting – but maybe if you had seen what I have seen on earth, if you had witnessed the atrocities I have witnessed, if you had seen the tremendous heartache that has been caused on earth due to your unworthiness which can totally be transformed then maybe you would be ranting also? I am not here just to pick up the pieces, to calm and heal and comfort, why should I continue to do this when I know there is a simple solution to cure it once and for all? If you were me, and had seen what I had seen, and had felt the pain and the disappointment that all of you share over and over again, wouldn't you want to change it, help people to see that at least there is another choice, another way of being, another path. Wouldn't you want to at least try, even though you know that no one is going to listen because their ears have been altered, closed down so that they can only really hear the voice of misery. pain and shame. They cannot hear me, even when they think they do, they cannot accept that what I might tell them is real and true and having devastating consequence – they cannot hear me, because I have put the solution fair and square in their lap. It is do able, it is something they have control over, it is something that they can change for themselves, no government or dictator to blame, no society or cabinet on which to put all the responsibility, there is no 'what difference will one person make' for I have shown that within your own life you can make a very big and real difference. No you do not want to hear me, not because I am out on a limb, as everything I have said makes sense, you do not want to hear me, you do not want to acknowledge what I am telling you simply because you do not want to feel like you should or could do something.

You like thinking that you are powerless, you like believing that you are a victim, you like the comfort and the security of being blameless, no power, no control. Even though you spend most of your waking moments seeking as much power and influence and prestige as you can get, still when someone says here take it – you are a little taken back. Like children playing on an inside playground that is soft and padded and offers protection from any kind of hurt, are you enamoured by your powerlessness and meaninglessness. The very thing that is your burden and thorn, is the one thing that you have grown so accustomed to, that to conceive of more, of anything different is to say the least frightening, and terrifying. You like leaving it up to the politicians, then you can complain when they do something wrong, you do not want people blaming you, holding you accountable. This is why people in reality TV shows soon realise the benefit of going under the radar, of not being seen of not making decisions and not being a leader If you lead when you fall you are to be held accountable, and no one, wants that – you like your invisibility, you like not having responsibility, this way you could quite easily continue to your death simply spending the rest of your days projecting and blaming others. This is easy – this makes your complicated life appear a little easier – a little smoother – you can just continue to stick your head in the sand and not have to worry about the consequence. But, at the end of the day you are paying a much higher price than what you are aware and your society and world are paying a much higher price than what you are aware.

Coming to terms with the belief that you are unlovable does not make you more unlovable, although it may appear that way at first – it is what can set you free. When you can free yourself from the pain and the longing of this belief, you then become open and receptive to love, true love, a state of awareness which remains at peace no matter the circumstance or situation – this ability to be above and beyond the influence of everyday life is the core of love.

It may seem contrary but by accepting and looking at your unlovableness you open a space where a greater love and state of awareness can enter and penetrate your life. Without doubt is this invaluable, without doubt is this worth working towards and fighting for, without doubt is this the single most worthwhile pursuit that you can do within this life and time.

Thus, in the next chapter will we focus upon this even more concertedly, so that you can begin to free yourself from the constraints and chains that this sense has imposed upon you and your life.

What is Love? Messages from Mary on Love and Fulfilment

Maya

Chapter Seven – Do I Look Fat in This?

Uncovering Unworthiness.

Beloved Ones, I am Mary,

I come forward today to reveal to you things which to date you have not wanted to look at. I come to lead you directly to the source of much of your pain and uncomfortableness. I come to show you a way out from constant dieting, fasting, exercising, lifting weights, applying beauty products, buying expensive clothes that you cannot afford, cars you cannot afford, and homes you most certainly cannot afford.

I come to let you know that you are ok as you are – that you need do nothing to impress the universe, life, the heavens, the angels, for indeed are you loved and valued just as you are right here and now. The very fact that you are part of existence should be evidence enough of your right to be at peace within it – without having to criticise your hair, your body, your house, your clothes, your loved ones, and your lifestyle. Now more than ever before is your society placing added pressure on you to look and appear at your very best. If you do not then you are supposedly a failure, a loser, lazy, self-indulgent or grotesque even.

Many of the successful people on earth cannot stand to look at obese people, cannot stand to be with losers even if just for a few minutes while waiting in line at the checkout, they hate those who do not attempt to be their best, look their best, do their best. They admire success, money, attractiveness, beauty, thinness, any personal characteristic that they associate with this. When faced with the opposite they become anxious, irritable, upset, and even at times aggressive and hostile. The reason for this is obviously they cannot stand to be around anything which reminds them of what they once were, or maybe even what they still perceive themselves to be on the inside. All of you fall into this category somewhere, you hate what you inwardly perceive yourself to be – that may not be losers necessarily – but arrogant, selfish, bad tempered or controlling, most of you will repeal from those who you perceive are like this.

Yet, your unworthiness still lies hidden within you, even when you encounter losers, rejects, obese people, failures, hillbillies, people who you think are not educated enough, aware enough, good enough, involved enough, evolved enough. You just accept that it was the person who you encountered who made you feel this way, not the feeling itself. Meanwhile this feeling lies hidden within you and you are then destined to enslave yourself to ridiculous work hours, career goals and objects, just so that you can prove to some invisible force, or someone in your life that you are not a loser, a failure, unworthy, unlovable.

This is why your goals do not give you the satisfaction and content that you imagine they will, as no one or no achievement can undo this sense within you that you are unlovable and unworthy unless you are prepared to look at it. So all of your intended glory will be empty will be hollow, will be lack lustre, or temporary at best, as ignoring the belief and seeking outer gratification to prove the inner belief wrong is futile and meaningless. While the belief remains within you are you held hostage to it day after day regardless of what you achieve, how famous you are, how loved by your peers or fans, or friends, underneath you cannot escape from this treacherous sense that nothing you ever do is going to be good enough.

Thus, while you remain intent on proving your worthiness everything that you do is meaningless and will feel worthless, until you correct the problem, go within and face head on this sense of unlovableness which more than your breath, your hair, your clothes, or family are a part of you. While you place greater meaning onto the things that do or don't occur in your life, so that you can evade this sense of unlovableness, are you then rendered impotent and powerless against this force. When you accept that outer circumstances do not influence or change any inner belief that you have, you then begin to take your power back, see things as they really are, clear your slate, and be able to slowly work towards a sense of self which is genuine, authentic, balanced and in harmony with life and who you are.

While you keep avoiding this, are you doomed to suffer the consequence of feeling out of the loop, not good enough for your friends, or colleagues, not a good enough parent, not a good enough lover, wife, husband, or worker and this has consequence day after day, moment after moment each day in your life for the remainder of your days. Authentic and real reward for effort can be gained, can become part and parcel of your life when you see things as they really are. When you acknowledge that no amount of career success can help you to feel more worthy or lovable, when you can accept that no amount of money can make you a more worthwhile person. When you can see how irrelevant money and success are to your inner health your state of mind, they begin to lose their power over you, and this is a good thing. When you can stand back from having to earn lots of money or even more money when you have let go of the need to gain a better position, or have greater leverage or power at work, you can refocus onto that which is important your state of mind, your inner health.

When you can do this, you will eventually learn that you can improve or change your state of mind regardless of what is occurring within your life. When you can see this, and when you can actually do it you automatically begin to take the enormous emphasis that you have on money and power off of it, back onto the simple things, how you feel, how others around you feel, how good it is just to be outside in nature, breathing fresh air, under a tree, watching the clouds etc. If you can accomplish just this, you will have changed your life, for the better.

For there is a world that exists away from and apart from the hankerings of society, from the hankering for money, for social activity, for sexual dalliances, for important happenings and gossip, for more clothes, for sport success, for leadership opportunities – all this fades away when you ground yourself within and become authentically aware of who you are. Then life is not so much about having and getting, discussing and planning, it is more about just being here, just enjoying the day, the air, the sun even if you are doing nothing, even if you are not doing anything exciting, even if no one important rings or contacts you. Every day is full of moments waiting for you to open them up and see what simple pleasure and sense of wholeness waits.

But you cannot see this, you cannot even sense this, as you have grown too familiar with having and getting, and all that this means, you need to keep up with the status quo, you need to attend to your work, you need to do what you must to get you where you want to go, only when you get there can you be free, or so you think, nothing else, nothing else but what you have decided upon can offer you freedom, happiness and the ability to be able to just let go and relax, and simply enjoy. But this is not the case, the rainbow you are chasing does not have a pot of gold at the end, and it will be years before you realise this truth.

Some people seem content with their successes, seem enlivened and enamoured by them – but this is only because they deny what is going on within them and focus instead on what is happening outside of them. They can then find a multitude of reasons to be happy as they remind themselves that they have a good job, a great car, wonderful friends etc. etc. even when this may not be exactly accurate. Yet, as they focus only on the outer, and rarely let themselves feel their inner world, they seem happy enough. But the day will come where they come face to face with their inner world, their disappointment and frustration, depression and sense of unworthiness and then my dear ones their lives will come crashing down around them.

Those who are naturally more in tune with their inner world, and cannot as easily suppress emotion may appear to have a harder time, but in the end these people develop much better coping mechanisms and strategies and this will make a difference towards the end of their life. The ability to be honest with oneself should be revered more amongst your society, as it assists greatly with the ability to be flexible with life, and adapt. The less honest you are with yourself, the less likely you are to adapt to change and uncertainty.

The greater ability you have to go within and seek to uncover your unworthiness the more worthy you will begin to feel. Most of you say you do not like going within as there is nothing there, you come up against a wall of thoughts which distract you into daydreams and memories, and thought associations which seem to go nowhere. But you can carve a path through this you can pierce beyond the veil of thought and once you do you will see exactly what I am speaking about. You will discover the 'eternal sky of mind' the spaciousness and openness that exists within you. This spaciousness that lies within you can prove to be a sanctuary for you in your hour of need, if you turn to it regulary remember it and seek it out, it will in your hour of need offer you comfort, clarity, security and peace. Enormous peace exists within you, enormous joy and bliss and love, you just have to want to find it, you need the motivation to find it, and persevere with it. There is no doubt of its existence and just because your culture has not shown you how to find it does not mean that it does not exist. Ask a Tibetan, ask them if they know about the 'eternal sky of mind' ask them if they have experienced spaciousness, openness within them, and you may be surprised.

Perhaps if the Tibetans had sought to be world leaders this would be more commonplace within your society, more frequent or discussed, but as the Tibetans do not value outer power or control of course in the race for world domination they are coming pretty close to last. Others instead invade and persecute them, because their strength is within, is gentle, and appears easy to override and dominate. Yet, ultimately their inner focus and calm makes them able to withstand atrocities which would decimate other cultures, and overall these beings have the ultimate victory, the ultimate attainment, which is held so close to them that you cannot see it, but it pervades them, nourishes them, and sustains them throughout.

If you can accept that perhaps other cultures have found this formula for spaciousness within it may be easier for you to accept that you too can also find this. Just because you have little awareness of it, or that it is advertised so little does not mean that it does not exist. More and more is your western society turning to the wisdom of the East, of Tibet, and if you can truly work with and digest the essence shared by these beings your society as a whole will be fortified and enamoured by the relationship.

The time has come for you as a species to delve within to find the luminosity that exists there, you have already discovered and explored most of your planet, your wilderness, your environment, you have gone as far into outer space as you are likely to get, and you have polished industrialisation and technology into gleaming works of art. The only place left for you to discover lies within, and without question what you find here will dwarf all of your other pursuits.

The benefit of going within can only be measured through experience, so I am now going to provide for you an exercise to help you feel your unworthiness, and by feeling it you will set part of it free. The more often you do this the better you are going to feel and you will find yourself for no reason at all being and feeling happy. Happiness is after all your natural state of being, it is not something that needs to be attained or worked at. Please work with the following exercise so that you can understand how potent this force of unworthiness is within your being.

Unworthiness Tour

Please either lie or sit down in a comfortable position, close your eyes and just feel the relaxation that comes from closing your eyes.

After a few deep exhalations, focus your attention on your solar plexus region between your rib cage and belly button. Try and put as much of your consciousness as you can into this region, so that it begins to enlarge and dominates your awareness.

Then have the intention of seeing and feeling your unworthiness, you could say 'I allow my unworthiness to come forward' or 'show me my unworthiness' or 'how do I feel unworthy'.

Just follow and allow whatever surfaces to surface – do not dismiss anything, and trust that what comes forward is for your benefit.

You may hear or see a phrase like 'I am ugly' or 'I never do anything right', or 'I am of no use to anyone', any self-critical thought that surfaces is attempting to show you an aspect of your unworthiness.

The main thing here is to not run from it, ignore it, dismiss it, or undervalue it, as your mind may attempt to lead you away at this point, not wanting you to penetrate this further.

Just keep focused onto this phrase, and the feeling that may accompany it, and just allow yourself to be here with this thought, just share the space with this thought. You do not have to reject or dismiss the thought, just be here with it. This may be uncomfortable in moments and you may want to run, to stop, to go onto something else, but it is pivotal that you just allow yourself to be here amongst this sense of unworthiness.

If you need to breathe into the phrase and feel it expand, feel it becoming larger, if you are game so that you can really feel its essence and energy.

The longer you can just stay here with this thought and feel it and not have to change it or run from it the better off you will be, as you will be pricking a part of its balloon so that it slowly can deflate over time. You may however at first be only able to stay here for a moment or two. This is ok, but remember to return often until you can withstand being here for quite some time. The longer you sit with this the better.

The more often you complete this exercise the more self-critical thoughts you will find, and as you learn to just sit with each one you develop a resilience to them which eventually helps to overthrow them from your being. When you are familiar with these thoughts you will more easily recognise them and see them clearly when they surface within your mind during everyday life. If you can see them throughout the day, you will then be more aware of what they are attempting to do and rather than give into them, and let them induce moods of lethargy, depression or anxiety you can choose instead to discount them and see them for the frivolous meaningless inaccurate thoughts that they are. This will with time empower you, and free you.

This simple process which does not seem overly complicated or difficult is what stands between you and your ability to feel good within life. This is the silent force that stands in between your entire communications making you feel as if the other person is attacking you when they were merely making an honest observation. This is the filter that insists that you take remarks personally rather than just letting them go as the meaningless chatter that they are. This is the bridge to your childhood which forces you to take each action of your spouse as badly and as naively as you interpreted the actions of your parents all those years ago.

As you begin to unhinge this link or bridge between the everyday and your sense of worthlessness, you will notice greater space within your mind and within your being. Instead of having ranting, incessant thoughts about one particular topic, the thoughts are fewer, the openness more luminous and easy to access, and you can then see the advantage clearly of going within. The hidden Mt Everest that you have as yet to uncover, the wonderful snow-capped peaks, the sheer height and clarity, freshness and aliveness that you feel here is indescribable to the people who have never been.

I promise you it will not occur overnight, but it will happen, if you work with this exercise, if you are sincere and authentic in your approach to it, it will work for you, it will work wonders for you. It can offer you something that going to the movies, shopping, chocolate, dining out, or even a romantic weekend away from the kids cannot offer – it offers you a new perspective and sense of connection to your life, where you are right here and now.

Only through this will you be able to face the things you need to face within your life, with dignity, courage, clarity and humour. Otherwise you will fall apart when your son goes overseas to war and be fearful and afraid day after day with no escape from the torment, the fear that he will not return. Or when your daughter drops out of college starts dating a drug addict, and does not want to see you anymore, when your parents health decline to such an extent that you must consider taking them on, having them at home with you, or at least check in on them constantly, if you are to be free of guilt and shame. All these circumstances and more are possibilities within your life – your daughter may become depressed after giving birth to her first child, she may expect you to look after your grandchildren more than you envisaged – your son may tell you one day that he is gay, your sister may become addicted to anti-depressants, your brother may lose his job and go through a midlife crisis, your brother in law may start drinking too much, and you may have to watch the hurt and the sadness, the disappointment in your nephews eyes. Your daughter in law may start sending you abusive e-mails. All these and more may still await you and how are you going to cope and continue without falling into atrophic addiction or compulsion yourself? How can you guarantee yourself that you can move on in a positive direction without turning to the bottle yourself, without feeling the need to work too often, or sleep too often, or veg out in front of the TV too often. Let alone call on your resourcefulness, compassion and courage to overcome these constant barrages of pain, and shame, guilt and hopelessness.

On the outside you can pretend many things, on the outside you can certainly satisfy yourself that you are doing the right thing, have a good life, will be able to meet these hurdles unscathed, simply because you distract yourself constantly from how you really feel and what is happening within you. And it is normally only once something is right in front of you within your life that you pay it any attention. You like to avoid the uncomfortable and this leads to denial. But, sure enough life will hit you, will throw rocks at you, as the Universe is an omniscient force that knows what you need within your life moment to moment, and each and every circumstance within your life which provokes dread and fear and guilt is really only trying to help you see the beliefs and the unworthiness that lays hiding within you.

When you consider the extraordinary lengths the Universe must go to show you on the outer what you have hidden on the inner, you can begin to glimpse at the true majesty and magnificence of this platform. Forget the wondrous mountains, hills, valleys and waterfalls, forget the Amazon, the Sahara, Madagascar, do away with all this and still your earth this platform, this world, this universe is so wondrous, so insightful, co-ordinated, detailed, complex and thorough that it makes even your greatest thinkers, look sheepish and impish. Each and every moment the universe is bringing to your door exactly what you need to feel the resonance of the beliefs, memories, emotions and fears hidden within you. Like a multidimensional jig saw puzzle that appears to have never-ending doors and passageways to link up people, circumstances, thoughts, emotions, events and memories at exactly the right moment so that you can not only follow your destiny, but feel everything that you want to avoid, is miraculous, ingenious, and heavenly in its design and complexity. And yet still the idea of me being able to transmit messages through a human appears like a science fiction fantasy? Yet astounding miracles are occurring all around you moment to moment without your awareness.

Someone that you dreamed of a day or two ago suddenly rings you up out of the blue, although you have not heard from them for ages. You run into someone who you haven't seen in ages and all of a sudden you remember events that took place years ago, things you haven't thought about for years, then you have an urge to contact another friend from this period in your life, and when you do you instantly gel, you meet, the old friendship is reignited you discover many similarities within your lives, and all of a sudden you are discussing going into business together, travelling together, dating each other….

As you continue within this relationship memories come flooding back, you start to remember what was important to you while you were young, you rekindle this passion, and it's as if you take on a new life. Other people have brief encounters with people who are linked to friends in their history, flooding back emotions and memories from that era, forcing you into a type of reminiscing which evokes memories, dreams, hidden ambitions, desires, yearnings, all so they can be released and set free from within you.

The lights play up at the intersection, you are late for an important event, and you criticise yourself and the lights endlessly, the reel of self-criticism begins and you are tormented by it for the remainder of the day and night, you cannot get to sleep, you toss and turn, there seems no escape from these blasted thoughts. Yet, if the lights hadn't of played up, if you hadn't of gotten a continuous stretch of red, then these thoughts would never have come. Thus are you forced against your will even to contemplate these thoughts, and many people make changes or a decision because of them, when in truth all that is needed is to see them.

Life is working with me, and against your pre disposition to want to run from your inner world – like it or not I have life on my side – my arguments are directly linked and related to what is happening within your world and life and being. I am not speaking of airy fairy faraway places that you will never reach within your mind, everything that I am speaking about is already within your life, within your mind, it's just you are stubbornly refusing to look at it and see.

But you cannot beat life, you cannot beat the energy of the universe that is bringing all these instances, memories, insights together for you, so that you can see yourself more clearly – if you continue to run and run you will literally be painting yourself into a corner – you will be butting your head up against an invisible brick wall time and time again. You cannot defeat life, you cannot overpower, outwit, outplay the universal life force – if you think you can you are foolish, blind or severely overestimating your own capabilities.

Like it or not this is what your life is about, being able to accept and learn from the situations that life throws at you. It is not about doing good works, obtaining people around you that love you, it is not about becoming a ceo, a millionaire, it is not about raising good kids, it is not about finding happiness or peace, it is not about some calling or purpose that you think you may have, just because you are good at something, just because you like doing something does not mean necessarily that this is your calling- you can easily indulge these activities in your spare time within your home, just for the love of it, not for what it can do for you.

You have exploited everything and everyone into a way to make money, a way to become successful, famous, revered within your community, and the more emphasis you place on this the more you lose touch with the innocence and purity that just enjoying these activities for the sake of enjoyment brings. You have corrupted every aspect of your society, you have polluted even that which was pristine and clear. You have corrupted even childhood, you have forbidden children to play their innocent games, you have brought in video games, early learning, you are expecting them to read younger, you are expecting them to add and subtract younger so that they can be at the top of their class, as somehow this will make their life easier?

You have corrupted everything that you lay your hands on, you have made even your pets some god like messiah who you treat far better than any human member of your family as your pets can't talk back, they seem to do what you want, they are obedient and needy, and as a result you swoon to them, adore them, you cannot leave them alone by themselves for god forbid that they should get lonely. So you buy toys, food, other pets for them so they are not lonely, you have corrupted and polluted even this. Nothing in your world is untouched by the pollution of your mind, your mind is so out of whack that you distort and destroy everything in your life. Yet remain oblivious to what you are doing, it seems natural and normal to you because everyone else has drunk from the same well of insanity and are doing the same as you. This does not make what you are doing normal or sane or beneficial, it just means all of you are mad.

To truly understand how out of whack your modern western society has become you need to go to impoverished countries to see how normal, simple people live. But, you are corrupting even them, TV's and computers which are considered mandatory for satisfactory human life are corrupting even them. There is no length that you will not go to to ensure that what you are doing is deemed normal.

Yet even amongst all this distortion and out of balance way of life, the universal force is still able to work and to throw back onto you all your fears and inner resentments that you have not been willing to see or deal with. If anything should prove to you the wonder of the universe that you live within it should be this. To think that you have corrupted what was natural and good and balanced within your earth and life for something which is plastic, is lopsided, demeaning and suffocating and still the universe can hit you with everything that you refuse to look at is significant, and surely proves to even the most closed and narrow materialists, that there must be something more than what the five senses can reveal.

In truth it is not even that the five senses cannot reveal higher realities, or grander vibrations within your environment for they can, you just don't use your five senses to their full capacity and it is this which prevents you from being able to see and to feel and to benefit from the higher frequencies within your environment. If you were to truly open your ears up, your eyes, your taste, your sense of touch and smell you would see that there is more surrounding you than what you realise. The fact that you have not been taught to do this, is a reflection on the plasticity of your society more so than the limitation of your senses or the falsity of higher vibrations existing.

Your scientists know that higher or different vibrations and frequencies exist, all of you know this, you learnt it at school, but somehow this gets lost in translation – you simply forget amongst the busyness of your important life, and besides what does that have to do with anything anyway you may respond. Yet, you feel for the blind child who cannot see the variety of colours surrounding him and available to him if only he could see, the glorious colours of a sunset on a hot summer evening, the beautiful clear blue of the cloudless sky, the beauty of a Monet, or even what he himself can draw, or the deaf boy who will never get to hear Mozart, Chopin, Lady Gaga, Aretha Franklin or even the waves crashing on the beach, the birds morning chirping session greeting the new day, he will never hear the soothing sound of his mother's voice, his sisters laugh and giggle, all this you pity him for, all this makes you sad, makes you feel compassion and pain, and yet when I explain to you how more devastatingly have you stopped yourself from experiencing the pure joy, bliss and ecstasy that exists just inches above your level of thought, you deem me to be talking about weird hallucination type philosophy which has no relevance to you and your life.

What is Love? Messages from Mary on Love and Fulfilment

In the end it is up to you, you have free will, and like a blind boy who becomes increasingly sensitive to sound, have you become too sensitive to life, to the clock, to having to do, and you have equally become desensitised to what happens within you, and around you, you have to otherwise you would be unable or so you think to honour your obligations to the clock god. If ever an invention should have been discarded it was this – for you have wielded this tool like a sword to sever your being and life into segments that may appear to fit and make sense to your narrow way of looking at life, but in the end will prevent you from realising your full potential and talent.

The security that time gives you is negated by the fact that it expects so much of you, it may help you to know where you are, where you need to be and what you need to be doing, and where others in your life are and what they are doing, but this security is a hallucination. This time slotting can offer you no real and lasting security it cannot stop an asteroid from crashing into the earth, it cannot stop global warming, it cannot stop twisters, tornadoes, tsunamis, it cannot stop your husband from flirting with every female that comes within his radius, it cannot stop your child from failing at school, it cannot prevent your hips and thighs from gaining a few pounds through winter, in truth the clock can offer you no guarantee at all – apart from knowing where people will be at any given moment. But even this is not a certainty, they could lie, they can easily decide to do something different, walk a different route, they could easily be meeting with friends who you dislike or loathe, the clock offers you nothing of substance, and if you were to look closely at the pros and cons of the clock you would deem him worthless and trade him in for something better within minutes.

But you simply have not taken the time to look and see what is going on – you simply don't have the time.

If by some chance that you might be thinking now that maybe you could make some time…..I am going to put forward an exercise based on one of your senses – hearing – so that you can see that what I am actually speaking about does have merit. I want you to realise that your senses can lead you to a higher awareness, they can be tuned to pick up higher frequency and vibration and that if this is the case, you can no longer argue that something must be factual, must be in the here and now for it to be real, for if you can sense it with your own ears, then it must be in the here and now.

Opening Up Your Hearing Contemplation

To do this exercise it may be helpful if you are at a beach, river, lake, stream or waterfall but if this cannot be managed being out in nature is going to be advantageous, somewhere where you can hear birds calling is ideal. If this cannot be managed then just sitting in your home is sufficient.

Sit in a comfortable position, gently and slowly close your eyes, take a few deep breaths just to help you relax and go inside. See yourself letting go of all the tension or activity from the day, as if steam is coming up and out of you allow everything that you have accumulated throughout the day to dissolve, and just let yourself be here in this moment.

If you start thinking about the clock what you have yet to do today, remind yourself that there is plenty of time and that in the grander scheme of things this is just a few moments out of your day. Tell yourself that you are allowed some 'me time' it is necessary and you deserve it.

Now place your attention and focus onto your ears and your hearing, just listen to the sounds coming into your ears. Focus purely on listening to the sound, do not judge or analyse the sounds or make comments about them or you may miss the next sound. Just listen to whatever sounds you hear within your environment. See if you can become the sound, your focus upon it is so all consuming. All your attention within it.

After you have done this for a few moments begin to extend your hearing and see how far away you can hear, really tune your ears to every possible sound that you can hear, without force or effort, this is something that you must relax into, like a hot spa, it is not something to race towards or force. Just be happy in the moment listening to what comes, if nothing else comes then so be it. Just keep listening, and keep your sole focus within your ears and hearing.

Now after some minutes begin to listen out for the gaps between the sound, taking your emphasis off the sounds that you are hearing and placing it upon the absence of sound. See if you can hear the gaps between sounds – for silence is actually louder and more penetrating than sound.

When you feel that you are getting the hang of hearing the gaps between sound, when you can sense silence, openness, spaciousness there – amongst the spaciousness or silence I want you to really attune your ears to this silence, I want you to really open up your hearing unto these gaps, like turning up the volume this should increase the sound of silence, I want you to really open yourself and your hearing up to these gaps. No matter how small, fleeting or hazy they may be.

Then I want you to take notice of what happens when you do. This is all. Remember your experience and promise yourself that you will repeat this exercise again within the next day or two.

If you can through this exercise see how you can access silence, you will see how my words actually mean something. Silence contains a higher vibration when you are within it there seems to be something very calming about it, very nurturing, the energy of silence *feels* different to your normal consciousness. It feels different as like infra-red, and microwave rays it is operating at a different frequency. Meaning that the atoms, chemicals, particles that make up silence are vibrating at a different rate, they are moving much faster.

Sometimes people experience a fluttery sensation when they are within silence, this is the effect of this more rapid vibration available here. The more you visit here the more accustomed you get used to it the deeper your penetration of it will be, this will expand your experience and the silence will get much larger, more frequent and more luminous. When you have experienced this, when you have had a taste of it, then my words begin to make much more sense, and have greater value and meaning to you. Thus just as opening up this book is important so too is working with the exercises contained herein.

You must give the exercises time to work, and give yourself time to adjust and get used to them and to be able to do them correctly. You cannot expect grand experiences on your first attempt – like all new skills you must practice. This is what all this is about re training your mind, re training yourself to look at life differently, re training your perception from that which is focused on the outside to that which is focused on the inner. When you can achieve this, when you are firmly planted in the centre of your being, many things begin to change for you, and around you. Suddenly all the drama's the high's and low's begin to smooth out, the peaks are not as high, the lows are not as low, and your awareness enables you to see beyond the peaks and the valleys, so that you no longer get so embroiled in them.

What at one time may have moved you to tears or anger no longer impresses itself upon you so thoroughly, there is a gap, it is no longer your sole circumference – you can preserve and nourish your inner world despite what is occurring on the outer. When you realise this, you feel as if you have been set free, as if a tremendous burden has been lifted off of your shoulders. Then what happens or does not happen within your life gradually becomes less and less important to you as you delve within more and more.

This is what true change is all about altering your perception your orientation 360 degrees – dropping a method of interacting and relating within the world that leaves you feeling on the left foot all the time for something which enlivens, nourishes and invigorates you. It then does not matter if you are not as involved with the outer life that you were once so heavily invested in. If you lose a few friends because of this new way of seeing then that also does not matter – if you are not invited out as often as you have chosen to stay at home more often than not this also is of little consequence. For at the end of the day, it is not how many friends you have in your life, it is not how popular you are, for love does not and cannot come from others if you cannot offer it to yourself. Just being able to be with yourself and sit with yourself will be far more valuable as you mature and reach your twilight years.

If you fear death now, if you are frightened of a million and one little things now, more than likely you are doing many of the things you are doing to avoid feeling this fear or having to look at it. As you age, as death gets slowly closer – the compulsion to keep yourself busy so that you do not have to think about things gets more and more demanding, and if you have lived your whole life this way – then you will feel compelled into action, into caring for others, looking after others, busying yourself with small activities, charity, etc. all so that you do not have to sit alone and sit and ponder the approaching death and disease. Grandparents then take on grandchildren, foster kids, they sign up to work for charities, or they indulge in relentless travel, touring, group activities to keep them active, feeling healthy and fit, so that they can pretend that death is still a long way off. Yet, this avoidance of the inevitable is not helping anyone least of all those who are about to depart. When death comes you would want to greet it with a warm calmness and serenity, an acceptance almost.

The more you fight it, the more you try and run from death the more difficult and arduous it will be. Leaving behind everything in this life that you have loved and needed and involved yourself with is of course a nerve wracking contemplation. Yet, when you can centre yourself within your own being totally autonomous of what occurs on the outer, you begin to see and realise that your own soul, the essence of who you are is central to your journey and path and whether you are in the body or not this soul, this essence within you cannot be extinguished. The more you feel, see and experience this, the calmer you will be as you approach death.

The more accepting of death that you are the more the 1001 fears that surface daily as a result of your fear of death no matter how young you are, will also begin to fade and lose weight and significance with you. Thus, just by learning this art of going within, of sensing silence within your mind and seeking ways to harness this, work with this, is going to be the best way that you can protect yourself against everyday fears. Being able to undo fear within your life, would have to be seen by many across many cultures, beliefs, religions or ages as one of the most worthwhile things that anyone can do – as this more than anything sets you free- lifts you up to a place where you can see and appreciate your full potential.

It is only because of your fear that you stay as you are, it is a direct result of your fears that you fail to take strides in the direction of your inner world. Also it is a direct result of your fear that prevents you from doing what you need to in ordinary life to feel happier, fuller, more alive and invigorated. Thus, fear is a substantial element within your life which potentially limits you to what you now are. No wonder you are not feeling fulfilled or happy, no wonder you are confused and overwhelmed all the time by what is happening within your life, and upon the earth? Your fears like a film layered across your eyes colour and filter everything you see, hear and do upon the earth. There can be no real freedom until such time that you remove this film of fear and see that indeed you have much within you, and within your life to appreciate and enjoy.

When fear vanishes from your sight, your world, you can see much more clearly what precious gifts await within as your connection to your inner world is more alive, clear and vibrant. It is a direct result of your fear that now appears to make the path seem hazy, unclear, muddy and uncertain. Once fear is gone, this path is effortless, but fear will not and cannot leave until you venture within despite the huge mass of fear and its consequence that you may encounter. Thus you are caught amidst a trap of damned if you do and damned if you don't. You have to assess the situation from your current limited perspective, and this is why beings like myself become important and necessary – for we assure you, guarantee you that you cannot fail if you earnestly commit to going within, and we promise you that indeed the gifts of going within will be numerous indeed, the first and most prominent obviously the ability to undermine and reduce if not eradicate altogether your fear and its consequence.

This is what will become more and more evident to you as you age, the tremendous amounts of things that you can fear – as death becomes more and more a reality fears become larger and more luminous leaving you feeling alone, and vulnerable against the force of a savage universe, clinging to what little you have your only protection. This is why so many minds falter, as the weight and the gravity of this fear overwhelms and almost disables ones capacity to think clearly and logically, leaving one with no recourse but to focus on the past as the awareness of what the future may bring too disturbing, too real and pertinent to contemplate.

At the end of the day your soul has ultimate power, you your inner essence has the ultimate choice and power to choose that which you will give into and that which you won't. Certain masters have tested the vastness of consciousness have tested its reliability and aim, some have deliberately put themselves under unnecessary burden, physical burden, pain, ridiculous situations whereby death could at any moment come, and in some instances where death should have come, but have been able to transcend it, instead riding on its coattails to an even deeper awareness and transcendence of death. Thus showing to them how reliable and potent their consciousness, their soul, their choice.

Thus, the feeble aged population that currently grows within your society is a direct result of your societies inability to teach and to show your populations a more real and authentic way of living and interacting upon the earth plane. A way of reinforcing soul and its power and effectiveness in and amongst the everyday – just by being more able to ward off dementia, illness, decay and atrophy. As the body ages naturally there are going to be consequences, but you are forgetting that in biblical times people lived to be 200 and

300 and sometimes even 400 years old. How could their bodies be able to endure these increased living spans? Was it just because there were less people on earth, less pollution etc. but then again they had no medicine, no medical technology like there is today. How did these beings live for so long? Was it just that they saw everyone else living to these ripe old ages and just believed this is the way it was, or were they more in tune with their essence, with their soul which has great strength, power and adaptability?

If you truly desire something, if you truly look for and want something then for sure it becomes more and more possible with each breath. Many people on earth have proven this within their own lives being able to attain things they never thought possible. Thus, the same must be true with death, you can approach death in a more consistent, enlivened, fearless manner which sees you becoming more and more in tune with who you are and the gifts that you hold rather than less and less in tune. You do have the ultimate choice as to where and when you die, there is no Angel of darkness or light coming to get you against your will, you have the ultimate power, this is why so many survive in incredible circumstances - pulled from debris weeks if not months after a natural event or tragedy.

This is why some people have been able to survive falling to the ground from 100's to 1000's of metres up, and is why some people can live to 110 without thinking twice, or can overcome serious illness and disease while others around them collapse and decay within a very short time. The very thoughts and choices that you silently make within your mind, the beliefs that you hold, all impact the way in which you will approach death or disaster. Those people who have had greater opportunities to experience and interact with a higher part of themselves, who have seen ways of moving beyond the limitation of normal thinking or who have adopted beliefs that enable them to rise above the normal status quo in a specific area, are easily able to do so. Those who have had fewer opportunities to feel the potency of the living force within them, who hold beliefs that they are a victim to life, are powerless, are unsafe or unprotected generally will fare much worse than others.

Thus, it will become essential for your society to recontact this force within you if you wish to be able to more easily deal and cope with adversity, ageing and death. What you are learning here are skills that all of you at some point will need to adopt if you are to have a better grasp on what is going on in your lives and why and how you can more easily overcome them. This is not some alternative therapy or belief system that only a few on earth will resonate to and be drawn to, this is your future.

Whether you choose to once again delay and delay until such time that you have nearly wiped yourselves off the planet, and then will you not out of choice but of necessity be forced into to working with these practices and methods, just so that you can survive and come to grips with what your lack of commitment to soul brings. Without soul in your life, without even the slightest awareness or care for it, you automatically sever yourself off from the life force the energy current of life which sustains nourishes and cares for you. You may not know any different currently, but if you had more role models, if you could have interacted with more enlightened people on your earth, you would see, that this life force, nourishes the mind, nourishes automatically what is important and quickly dissolves and destroys that which isn't.

Thus enabling greater clarity of mind, less confusion, indecision, wrong choices etc. so that your whole life path can flow much more smoothly, with less erraticness, or chasing your tail effect. Being able to tune into your inner essence, being able even to glimpse at your soul is one of those experiences that you will never forget. Soul is not just a term, which anyone can speak about, soul is an experience, and when you realise this, this is all you will want, this is all you will crave. All the thoughts about success, and money, love and good fortune will wither and fade immediately as the dawning awareness of soul enters your life. This is what will sustain you, this will make approaching death at any age simple and carefree, smooth and calm. This in turn will sustain and nourish your entire species. For you will be unable to move from where you are if you cannot accept the possibility of this. Now more than ever does your species need a new direction and this new direction must be one that is linked to your inner core, your centre, your soul.

Without soul you will continue to attract unhealthy thoughts into your mind, and energies into your body, and will then have to fight relentlessly with these forces which will inhibit and restrict your ability to move forward, and upwards, clearing a path for kindness, peace, calm and serenity. Only when this has become the staple of your diet, only when you can clear your energetic field effortlessly, only when you easily rise above the thoughts in your mind, can you begin to know and to feel the satisfaction and content that comes from wisdom, higher orientation, feeling, and clarity of mind. As you are you are doomed to a life of fighting everything and everyone who enters, and having to fight for every step forward that you take, which ultimately has invisible costs that impact you more severely than the step itself.

Life shouldn't be this hard, life can be easy, you just need to learn ways to get out of your own way so that you can allow the current of life to easily move you where you need to be so that you can gain the clarity of mind necessary for this. Not questioning anything is not flowing with life, it is hiding from it – not saying 'No' is not flowing with life it is allowing yourself to become a victim to it – not standing up for yourself is not being kind and loving and spiritual – it is the opposite, it is disempowering yourself, disconnecting you more from who you are, your innate instincts, responses, insights and senses. Following your hunches, your intuitions is all about flowing with your core, the more you can back yourself and bet on your hunches, the more you can trust and rely upon them the greater the opening within you, and the more you open, the more the current of life can work through you.

This then counteracts the beliefs of unworthiness that you hold within you, gradually creating greater and greater space whereby you can distance yourself from the unworthiness so that it need not impact you, move you, sway you and torture you the way it does currently. So that when someone makes an honest remark about your clothes, or work, children or husband you can shake it off like water off a ducks back, without it having to pierce so deeply your thin skin and create disturbance, fatigue and conflict within your life and being.

Even if you can only accomplish this much, imagine what difference this could make within your life, no longer over reacting to what others say or think, no longer needing others to approve what you are doing or not doing as you feel ok as you are, there is no inner unworthiness that you need to cover over, or console. Imagine the ripple effect of this, impacting and influencing your entire world, no more need to rush to be on time as it no longer matters what others think, being late cannot be used against you to make you feel bad as the unworthiness that this normally triggers has receded and vanished without a word. Not having to rush, just being able to take your time as you go about your day, fulfilling your daily requirements would mean your whole day takes on a whole new aspect, a whole new energy and rhythm. This rhythm may enhance your day bringing forward the roses so that you are more acutely aware of them and appreciating them as you walk by, not having to seek them out as something added on your to do list, just being able to soak in the goodness that each moment naturally offers regardless of whether you are at work, or at home or in between. Surely this perception is worth fighting for – surely this way of living is worth working towards – and most definitely too precious to ignore and walk away from?

What is Love? Messages from Mary on Love and Fulfilment

Maya

Chapter Eight – Love Revolution Receptivity.

Beloved Ones I come forward in the form of this book to help you to see another way of being and of interacting upon the earth. I see clearly what your inability to question your love brings into your life and world, and I know that this need not be. I am not asking you to abandon your love, I am only asking that you re decorate, and renovate it into something which is more satisfying real and permanent. The love that you currently believe in and trust is misleading you daily and you are allowing it to mislead you, you are allowing others to mislead and deceive you, betray and belittle you all under the banner of love. And you accept this, you feel powerless against it, as to do anything else does not fit under your banner of love. To look at your own wants and needs is considered selfish and conceited within this love, to want to change this, to want to do something for yourself is also considered selfish and unloving. Thus must you consistently put others first, forcing you to clean up your children's messes, pick up after them, protect them, clear their slate all so you can uphold this definition of love. This type of love then is more about control, which is advocating a generation of children who expect the world and are becoming less and less responsible for what happens within that world.

Love if it is to be worthwhile and valuable must at its core give all people their own power, without restriction or limitation on how they use that power. But, neither can it hide the consequence of power abuse or seek to make right what people or children unaware of the potency of this power do. If you are to offer back all people their own power through love, you must disconnect yourself from them and their choices, otherwise you will fall inevitably back into the trap of cleaning up after your children, and this as you must be becoming more aware of now, does not solve the difficulty of life it only exacerbates it.

If your children are to feel alive and centred within the core of who they are, they must take control of their own destiny, make their own mistakes, and learn the lessons provoked by these mistakes. Learning that every choice has a consequence is an important life lesson, the sooner it is learnt the easier other life lessons will be as they arise. Cleaning up after your children helps you to feel needed and wanted and necessary. Fulfilling this inner need within you is not love, but you have mistakenly thought it was love as it makes you feel good. You have learnt over time to associate these nice wholesome feelings of being needed as love, but this is an incorrect perception which has led to the downfall of a real and authentic love.

Love if it is pure, must free you from everything that you see around you, for love is the energy current of life which will lead you back to your original source. Love is an energy thus you will experience it as an energy, a feeling, something that appears to lift you up above the confines and limitations of need and obligation. Love when it is experienced will be pure love, in other words it will not be mixed with hate, resentment, ecstasy, bitterness and frustration. If you look at your love interactions to date, you will see that the majority of them invoke at least two emotions, not just one – not just love – you also may feel lonely as your perceived source of love is not there – you may also feel angry as they expect you to do something that you do not wish to do – if this continues you may start to feel frustrated, and this frustration may eventually lead into a form of depression or meaninglessness.

Authentic love differs significantly to that which you have learnt to perceive as love on earth. Authentic love is an energetic source which can transport you to other worlds, when with the love of your life you may feel as if everything is different, as if the world has transformed into a magical fairy land, but even this is limited and restricted compared to the very real energetic advantages offered by authentic love. Authentic love is not just something you do or offer someone else, it is a pathway to your higher self or soul. It links you to your multidimensional aspect, and enables a much broader comprehension of life. This is automatic not planned or attained through hard work, it just happens when you link to your soul, your higher aspect.

However, it is the linking to your soul which is the tricky part – until you do you are merely operating from the outer circumference of your personality, and as much as you may revere, discuss or think that you have attained some level of soul, you are deceiving yourself, for although you can attain glimpses of soul through inner contemplation within the outer personality, you cannot fully understand or appreciate its significance until you have pierced the seal that opens one up to soul. When this occurs you will never forget it, and you will have continual access to it thereafter, literally then transforming your life, and life path for the better.

Obviously being able to enter the inner sanctum, the inner caverns that contain soul means that you have to be a little bit like Aladdin, you have to be pure of heart, honest, and authentic, one must seek diligently to go within, or else lose the opportunity to find that which one is looking for. Many people have spiritual experiences, many people believe they have found something that they have not, and continue to believe in this even when they see evident signs that what they thought they had found is lost or gone. Spiritual experience has become a bit like an achievement now, with the Dalai Lama and Buddhism really opening its doors to the West, people are curious, and many have worked in a sincere manner to reach heightened levels of awareness within them. The very effort however, the very need to have to achieve, to turn this into some goal, disables or handicaps the seeker, for to truly experience heightened planes of existence you must become very very receptive and open – thus the value and importance of surrender. You must be able to let go, your whole being must be in an let go frame of mind – there can be no little weedy thoughts at the back of your mind continually assessing and analysing your experience and telling you 'no no this is no good, you are caught back up in your thoughts again'. For this shuts you down, breeds thoughts of failure and unworthiness and this then takes you down a route or path within your inner caverns which leads directly to frustration and hopelessness. Thus many spend years and years being frustrated with the spiritual aim and pursuit, and eventually have to make more of what they experience in a bid to keep up appearances at least for themselves.

Even though they may follow all the rules, not hurt anything, are peaceful and loving on the outer, when they go inside they become warriors and businessmen expecting the right outcome from applying the right formula, mantra, chanting, focus, following a set meditation regime, yet all the while they cannot see that this expectation, this intent is undermining their best efforts and receptivity. Openness is the key here – openness is a very simple concept and yet perhaps it is too simple, too easy to overlook, and perhaps too difficult to understand, for what exactly is openness, and how do you remain open continually amongst your meditation efforts?

Most meditators become fearful of thought, they avoid them, they think that if they see a thought that they have lost the battle, and are then frightened that they will become caught up in the thought dance, yet already just by being fearful of thought they have become caught in the current of fear which leads to a particular type of thought. This avoidance of one aspect, and embracing of its opposite can only work for a time. Both aspects must be embraced, both aspects seen to be equally as helpful if one is to transcend them.

When you look at thought, when you peer into it, you see that thought is a vibration it contains energy, this energy that exists within thought links to other energies within your mind, or within higher planes of existence, so you could equally alight to higher states by following these thoughts just as well as you can by standing back from them, creating space between you and them. Following these thoughts does not necessarily mean getting caught up in them, but certainly it means allowing them to be there. The idea that these thoughts should not be there becomes an obstacle itself within meditation, for the mind is going to interpret the energy contained therein, and if it is accustomed to using thoughts to do this, so too will it continue to do this. Fighting thought, trying to eradicate your mind of it, is going to be an arduous, extensive and almost impossible pursuit.

Only by allowing thought to be there can you transcend it- the art of course is to move back and away from thought, but even this can imply to a novice meditator that one should not indulge them, should exterminate them. Whereas the opposite is the case, if you are to overcome thought you must embrace it, you must open to thought, you must open to all energies within your mind, this is how you create greater opening, this is how you coax the higher energies down into your mind, and into your being. The thought will transform and transmute itself by itself into energy, just learning ways to embrace the thought rhythms of your mind without allowing them to disturb or impact or influence you is the key. If you can remain untouched, unscathed, unperturbed by the thoughts then their meaninglessness soon becomes apparent and they will of themselves wither and sneak off into the distance feeling the impotence of their form or figure. Thus, novice meditators should have within them this sense that the importance is not to be placed on thought or no thought, the emphasis is to be placed on how they respond to it. Opening to thought, embracing it, accepting it, neither trying to get rid of it, or follow it then creates within the meditator a reservoir of receptivity, and this receptivity is the fertiliser for all other encounters and experiences within the spiritual domain.

When one is able to stabilise this calmness, this serenity in the approach to meditation much can be gained in a very short time. When one see's and feels the significance of one's attitude toward meditation, life, higher or lower energies, then one automatically gains a very firm grip on the essence of openness and receptivity. Approaching all aspects of spiritual work in a calm and balanced manner, neither getting flustered or put out by incessant thoughts within the mind or unacceptable thoughts such as anger, jealousy, rage, one can then more easily transgress through them just through pure acceptance and an uncompromising faith in the goodness of all and everything.

In essence this approach to life will stand anyone in good stead no matter what the circumstance or situation that he may find himself within. When you can simply open to life, and just be in it, feel the goodness of it rather than the evil, when you trust life, and what it brings forward, with an awareness that transcends naivety, you automatically raise your awareness so that you have access to a clearer mind, a creativity which expresses itself in balance and formidable insight, rather than the normal chaotic impulses which deplete and ravage the ordinary mind and being.

Understanding that the breath itself that your approach itself is what will save you is instrumental in changing your awareness and perception of love. When you can move throughout life, with an open receptivity, when you simply stand amidst your anger, your restlessness, your fear, your jealousy, your unworthiness, your fear of humiliation, your fear of being ugly, unacceptable, your compulsion to work, to have sex, to drink, to eat, to shop, to watch too much TV, to do nothing but laze around, when you can just be with these compulsions and sensations, when you can simply allow yourself to be in the same space with these attributes, feelings, forces and not do anything just wait in the stillness and the silence of who you are, you begin to change the dynamics within you. You begin to loosen the grip that these forces have upon you, and when you undo these, you automatically undo much of the pain, hardship and difficulty in your life.

When you can learn to withstand the pull and the weight of these forces and not run in the opposite direction, just sit with them, have patience and understanding for them, you realise that you are the one with ultimate control. You are the one who chooses what you do, and how you act. You are the one with the say so, you do have ultimate power and control over your life, you just cannot see it now as you are not taking the time to see just how much power and control you do have. When you can learn to withstand these negative forces and compulsions, when you can learn to remain receptive to them, without giving in to them or following them, you dramatically loosen their power over you, and they will soon give up the fight for they will see that you can undo their efforts quite simply and easily, and when they see this it will not be long until their whole impetus and motivation is undermined and then you are free. When you give up these habits, or when these habits leave simply because you have shown them their powerlessness, they then can be replaced with something else. Hopefully, you will be strong and vigilant enough to ensure that they are replaced with their positive counterparts – love, awareness, silence, peace and calm. When this occurs, when your body and being automatically begin replacing past habits within you with these higher attributes, even without your full awareness, you will begin to see and to feel the very wonderful blessings that have been bestowed on you.

Now when you feel rushed there will be greater opportunity for you to stop and see that in truth there is no need to feel rushed, you will be able to bring the awareness of peace into your rushing, you will be able to if you choose bring calmness into your rushing, so instead of running around frantically, you simply walk decidedly calmly powerfully in the direction that you need to head, with a sense of purpose and a feeling of calm rather than a sense of dread and worry about all that there is still left to do. This inner feeling, this inner calm will nourish and support you, it will become the focus then amongst the rushing, amongst the list of to do things.

When your perception changes from what there is to do, what is on the outer, to how you feel within and amongst it all you automatically offer yourself greater power and freedom from the ordinary the mundane. This inner sense of who you are, is significant and is what all else must be based upon. Without the awareness of who you are, how you are feeling, you lose your point of contact with your source, your inner essence, your power, your dignity, your potency. This is why there is so much emphasis on feeling, as it is through your feelings that you discover who you are, your heart centre holds the key, only by transgressing through your feelings, not around them can you come to see and know the potency of who you are, and to that which you are part.

When you become seated within this centre of feeling, of how you are feeling on a daily basis, when you can shift your awareness to this, when this is at the forefront of your being, and it will occur naturally within the right time if you work with me and my methods – then you will get lost in your menial thoughts less, you will give into these menial thoughts less, and you will as a result gain greater insight into your life, into each moment of each day. Each moment, and it will begin with a moment or two here or there, and gradually increase to a few moments each day, then a few moments every few hours, and then one or two moments each hour, until it is fully integrated within you, and is there 24/7.

Then there is no need for effort, then techniques like mindfulness become irrelevant, the effort that mindfulness requires normally takes an extreme personality that is obsessed with achievement to attain. As I mentioned previously achievement and meditation do not mix, instead via receptivity, by remaining open and aware, by embracing all and everything, will you more naturally just fall into a dawning awareness that grows by itself. This naturally occurring spontaneous consciousness or heightened awareness is like having Tinkerbelle alight on your shoulder. These are gifts sent directly from the universe to you, they occur all the time, you have sectioned yourself off from them so that you cannot currently see or feel them, but they are occurring 24/7.

Gradually as your real sight begins to open, as your being becomes more and more open and receptive, these moments of feeling the potency of who you are, will get larger, broader, until such a time that they overtake you, they will become you, for you are they and they are you. Then you will see a side to yourself the likes you never imagined, then amongst seeming poverty, or isolation, persecution, or chaos, you know for the first time who you truly are, and why you are here – to discover this. Your higher self then no longer is above you, your higher self then becomes firmly implanted into you, overlapped, superimposed on top of you, until you melt like ice into him/her. Now your soul has been grounded, through meditation and spiritual experience combined with the groundedness of walking everyday day after day with a growing awareness of this inner you which is growing, which is becoming, which is actualising............

This is how you grow love into your life, for this heightened awareness is love, is your connection to love, seeing clearly is love, being aware and alert and empowered with your core essence is love. Without this there can be no real love, for your need your impoverished little egoic self demands demeans love and steals it for its own purposes and glory. Like Gollum from Lord of the Rings does he steal the ring of fire, and attempt to keep it all for himself, believing that through this does he become all potent and powerful, yet the acts he must commit in order to obtain and keep the ring, wrench from him and pollute any goodness that may be offered. Weakening him then, until such time that he can no longer hold onto what little he has and must forfeit the ring or die clinging to it.

So too does your love corrupt and pollute any goodness that may be contained within it. Only when you can begin to see the ways in which you act to obtain, sustain and maintain this love can you see how any goodness is extracted from it. For if love is to be love, it should induce actions and behaviours which correspond to it, and not only this, reinforce and extend it, not its opposite. You shouldn't have to argue with someone or beg someone to get them to stay with you, if you love them you must let them go, their happiness must be the priority. If you love someone then whatever makes them happy is of utmost importance – if they want to leave, you let them go, and you do so without tears or fanfare, you do so with love and gratitude in your heart for the love you have shared to date. So what if they have been sleeping with a girl half their age? If this is where they deem happiness to be, you must acquiesce, love demands this, and it should not be under sufferance that you offer it, it should be with joy and gratitude in your heart, because love can only come in abundance. Real love cannot be tamed or controlled or measured, it simply overflows, the person offering it has no more control over it than the person receiving it. This is how removed your love has become from what is real, you have all become ego centric in your love getting, you measure and calculate, you theorise, you stocktake what you have done for others compared to what they have done for you, you have all become little Hitler's in your own world.

Now is the time to see just how corrupt and polluted your love methods have been to date, and only by seeing this, and realising this, do you stand any hope of attaining its opposite. Only when you see the value in stopping selling your love, can you grasp its true meaning and significance. For while you feel you need others to love you, to prove your worthiness does the idea of not selling your love scare and confuse you. It will take much even, for you to admit that you have been selling your love to date, but I assure you, you have – 99.9% of the population sell their love, and attempt to buy love from others. This is what you have been taught, you do not know any different, and each generation slowly slowly is getting greedier and more corrupt in their bid to buy love. This is why it must stop and it must stop now, before you destroy yourselves with this imbalanced, out of kilter perception of love.

Love from the outside to you looks like cuddling, hugging, kissing, smiling, touching, having sex, being happy, getting along with people, a sense of harmony and satisfaction pervades. When you buy love this is what you are hoping to get, this is what you are buying the images that have been put forth on your TV and movie screens, books and plays, role models, what you think other people have about love and what love is. You decide first and foremost who you deem worthy of your love, and more importantly whose love you want the most, particularly in regards to romance, but parents will also deem one child more lovable than the others, the one that displays characteristics that the parent holds in high esteem. Uncles and aunts will do the same, sisters and brother's cousins and friends will all choose and select and spend more time with, be closer to those who seem to display characteristics that the purchaser holds in high esteem.

Thus children and people who display positive characteristics and are seemingly more lovable, better looking, more palatable will generally feel more loved than children or people who do not display these characteristics and features. These people will normally not have as great an urge to prove themselves, or would be willing to do as much to earn love or buy love as it just seems to be there. Particularly good looking people will most likely go in the opposite direction, not feeling that they need to do anything for anyone to buy love, instead they will focus on selling what they have, their goods, their love as they have seen and realised that they are valuable, worthy, lovable, and will use this will sell what they have to get them their version of love.

Others who feel less loved, will feel they need to do more to earn this love, thus they may become very very good at something in order to earn love, respect, appreciation. They will work hard to become valuable and then they will feel like they have something to offer, something to sell. By working in this regard they are earning love from either a parent, sibling, partner, or they are hoarding their gifts to sell at a later date to someone who they deem worthy.

Others who may have grown up with more attractive siblings, smarter siblings, stronger siblings, more athletic siblings, or siblings that seemed to do better than them, will or may then go in the opposite direction, they may rebel against love they may despise this hierarchy which makes them the losers, and even if they have the unfaltering love of their mother or father, still the one parent who disapproves of them, may make them rebel going seemingly off the rails, in a bid to show that they don't care that they have lost. If they see that by going off the rails significantly they make their parents feel guilty, or even show greater care and love for them, then they will continue with this, either as a means of getting back what they believe was taken from them, or withheld from them, or as a means of punishing those who withheld it.

Thus your society is sliding down a very slippery slope – the more emphasis you place on this love that can be bought and sold, the more you undercut and undermine everything else that you do here. All your charity work, saving and caring for animals, orphans, sexually abused children, beaten children, the homeless, the weak, frail and needy – your attempts to be more environmentally friendly, green technology, creating sturdier economies, more jobs, more opportunities, finding out what particles existed at the beginning of time for earth are all undermined by your inability to offer a real and genuine love, which is not forced, or calculated.

Your love undermines these aspects of your lives as this lack of feeling loved that you are cultivating on mass is the very substance and force that induces extreme emotion in people, anger, rage, frustration, sadness, fear, concern, worry, viscious impulses, a non caring attitude, for people believe that if they have not had a good life, why should anyone else, it is just the way things are. The people who drug and enslave young Cambodian girls into the sex trade, have themselves been treated this way so they do not see that they are doing anything wrong. Their parents sold them, so selling other young girls is almost normal, there is no conscience telling them this is wrong, this is all they know, this is how you survive.

In the same way politicians go to work after fighting vehemently with their wives or children, feeling out of sorts and isolated, compelling them to speak aggressively or be uncooperative more so than normal within their normal discussions. If there are a few politicians feeling the same, this may mean a certain bill does not get passed, or others are unnecessarily put on the agenda as a result of this unclarified emotion motivating and compelling them in unseen ways everyday, every moment.

This unresolved conflict, this emotion which all of you have been trained to avoid at all costs does not simply go away because you are not looking at it. It may feel like it has for a time as you are distracted, but the energy remains there, and you will be at its mercy, it will suddenly drive you into anger when your son walks in the house with muddy shoes, it will make you drive faster, honk at people, and drive more erratically than normal, inciting or advocating accidents which dramatically impact and influence many peoples lives. Everything that is happening on your earth is happening because you are accepting this counterfeit love for the real thing. Only when this is corrected do you as a species have any hope at reconciling and curing the tremendous difficulties on earth. These problems will not go away one day, you will not be able to earn more, work harder, have so much information in your head that it almost bursts to fix your problems, as the roots are growing deep under the earth and are encroaching upon the footing of your house. All the while you are painting the roof, and the walls in a bid to make the house look better thinking that this will cure your essential problems, but never really even looking once to where the actual problem lies – within you, within all of you.

Now is the time for you as a global community to see and to know that to continue to evade your own consciousness in a bid to forget, in a bid to be rational, and normal, productive and sane is not working. Psychology exists for a reason, yet nowadays unless you are unable to work due to a mental health concern you run from it, and even when you do seek help you are merely put on anti depressants or medication, told to exercise and relax, thus leaving the mess that lies within you raging uncontrollably.

Meditation even is useless unless it is used as a means of connecting you with how you really feel. Yet, the stigma associated with the spiritual realm, and the boredom and stuffiness associated with meditation, creates the idea even that meditation is a goal, another thing on your long list of to do things. Not something that you can enjoy and use to guage your feelings, your fears, beliefs and actions, no it is simply another chore, you must abolish thought – no wonder all of you are so confused and have no where to turn, even your useful avenues for transformation have been polluted and corrupted.

Meditation is not about achievement, it is not about getting somewhere that currently you are not – meditation is about allowing yourself to be exactly where you are. As grossly as the Vatican corrupted religion, so too are your meditation experts and gurus corrupting the spiritual path and aim. Some of them do this unwittingly, others do it intentionally, but nonetheless meditation and the way in which it is taught has been severely corrupted and distorted, making it a much more arduous task than what it actually is. Your intellect which likes puzzles, gravitates to this secret maze or passage type scenario, this meditation complexity which would spoil and deflate even the most courageous of spiritual warriors. No wonder you all settle for clairvoyance – meditation has been turned into some ascetic, unnatural discipline, that can be attempted only by those with a sadistic inner force that likes punishing themselves for the pursuit of happiness. Can you see the contradiction here? Mind transcendence sounds complicated, and as you are all so unaware of what goes on within your mind it seems fair enough, that transcending your mind could entail uncomfortable postures, neverending sitting, fasting, depriving yourself of everything that you enjoy and love in a bid to somehow climb over the wall of your mind – yet this attitude is taking you in the direct opposite direction to your own unique inner path.

If you really knew the essence of meditation and transformation you would see that it comes through absolute ecstasy and bliss, reverence and abundance – not the other way round. Not excruciating pain, uncomfortableness, and exhausting hours meditating in a bid to tame that which is evil, base, or the opposite of goodness, your spiritual essence within you. The idea that you can contort yourself into some gymnastic meditator all the while supressing and suppressing and ignoring your inner feelings in a bid to overcome them is foolish if not ridiculous to say the least.

If meditation cannot connect you with how you really feel of what good is it? If meditation is only going to force you into even greater suppression of how you feel in a bid to overcome thought, then it has no value, and you are actually better off not doing it at all. Love is what you are seeking, either in life or meditation, love is the core or should be at the core of your search. You saw first hand the negative impact of Ghandi's version of love – non violence – all else must be supressed in a bid to uphold the moral law and attitude of non violence. Thus non violence is equated with some spiritual etiquette which is lost on me – as this approach to be non violent at all costs may have freed India from English rule, but did little to free its people from hatred, violence and anger – as it was supressed even more greatly it would surge up then in ridiculous fighting and violence thus severing the muslims from the hindus, creating two countries out of one Pakistan and India, who to this day still hate each other so intolerably, that they are considered by some to be a major nuclear concern.

You cannot force love – you cannot demand it, neither can you expect or demand spiritual liberation or etiquette – to do so is to greatly underestimate and de value the essence of love, the quality and aroma of it. If you are to change your thinking and the thinking of your species you must be courageous enough to look at your staples, your pillars that you take for granted and to evaluate if they are actually assisting or detracting from your overall environmental health. I know that this information may come somewhat as a shock to you – I know the very idea that your love is somehow polluted or false may cause emotion to flare up for no reason at all, but until you can face the truth there will and can be no genuine change on earth.

This is why I have to come, if I did not have to come, if it was not utterly essential that I come to assist for sure I would have preferred to remain the aloof, mysterious, comforting figure that appears suddenly amongst crisis or despair. But, I have seen enough of your grief and despair now to know that the solution will not and can not come from humanity alone – some help is needed, for you are all swimming in the same soup of earth vibrations which enabled the Vatican to turn religion into a business, that enables world wars and invasions without cause to continue to this date, that supports and nourishes child abduction, pornography and abuse simply because you are so inept at addressing the cause of these injustices.

You cannot see that it is all psychological, it is all energetic, it is all emotive, until you see that you are bypassing your cure each and every day simply by remaining busy, forgetting to think about things that matter and delve deeper into them, and upholding a continuium of love which is ineffective and detrimental, will you continue to slide downwards on this very slippery slope. Now is the time for action, now is the time for a love revolution, now is the time to question how valuable your love is that you are working to attain.

When you can turn your perspective around from a love that you have to buy or coax, to keep those whom you deem lovable in your life and content with you, or saving your precious love for those who earn it, when they earn it, to a broader love which encompasses all and everything and comes only to those who can let go of morality, inhibition and sanity in favour of that which they love that which is fun, that which comes from within, then you will see how easily and simply your whole way of living can be turned around, and transformed.

Love if it is to be real must have effect within you, it must make you happy, love and happiness are the same, there is no division or partition. Love does not and cannot induce misery pain, resentment or bitterness. Love is allowing yourself freedom to follow to the smallest tee that which you want and feel good with, only by doing this can you avoid suppression, and only by avoiding or side stepping suppression or repression can you offer others in your life the freedom to do the same without regretting it, holding them responsible for it, or seeking to have them repay you for it.

Only when you set yourself free can you offer this same freedom to others, only when you are free can you know and experience love. Love is an abundance that comes like a flower or a fruit upon a tree or plant. It comes simply because it has been unimpeded, it is allowed to grow anyway it likes, even if it is trimmed or trained it seeks to twist and turn to the light so that it can receive the natural goodness it requires for its optimal health and longevity. The plant or the tree does not allow anyone or anything to stand between itself and the sun, itself and the earth, itself or water, if it did it would perish. It naturally grows towards and seeks these elements, there is no stopping this natural process, or else the plant surrenders to death.

As a result of this firm resolve and trust in the elements that sustain it, the plant grows forward expediently, happily, frutitiously. The plant is happy, it has sun, air, water, soil and nutrients, it then glistens in the morning sun, blows rhythmically amongst the wind, and offers spontaneously and effortlessly rich, luscious, juicy fruit or flowers. It does this for no reason, it is not trying to feed a family, a village, a species, it is not trying to delight someone with its color or scent, it is not trying to pollinate and germinate and propagate other plants insects, species. The plant or tree cares about this not at all – the plant just likes growing and glistening in the sun, letting go and dancing with the breeze, opening to the night sky, the moon and stars, and surrendering to the vibration of energy engaged all around it. This is the way it is supposed to be, no care or thought of the other, just letting go into what is – this is love.

Thus the fruit comes forward out of this union between all these elements, it comes forward naturally and effortlessly, it just happens because this energy, this mixture of elements creates a concoction of love and creativity, and fertility, sprouting new life, growth, fruit and flowers. This is love an abundance, a result of just being, of not trying to be anywhere else. This is the only true form of love, it can never be guaranteed or a sure thing, sometimes the fruit will not come, or will not come in abundance, the elements may have withered, the soil may be dry, not enough water, the sun too hot, and what does come may be smaller, drier, less juicy, not worth eating. For just the right amount of these elements are required to create this balance, this love, this energy of abundance. If the amounts and timing are not right, then love cannot come and will not come….. there is and can be no guarantee…

This is why you have abandoned this love, this is why you have forsaken it for something more secure, more stable and certain, for you do not like uncertainty, one day your girl may love you the next she may not, who knows? Love cannot be manufactured and sustained by force, sin, repentence or marriage, just because you form a family, does not guarantee love, does not secure it. You have experienced this and are aware of it on some level, but you refuse to admit it, to sit with it, to see it fully for you know not what else you can do. You do not realise how real love feels, you do not know what you need to experience true and real love, for its dimensions and elements can be as invisible and simple as air, and water, and what is hiding within the earth. You then must look for it and must not in your ignorance search in a rushed or scattered manner or like a bull in a china shop you may unwittingly extinguish that which you are looking for.

Thus has your society unknowingly wiped real authentic love off the side of the planet, occasionally it occurs here or there, but it is so rare that to say it exists and that everyone sees it would be to mislead you again. It is understandable, you did not really know what you were doing, you just followed along with what you were taught and shown while young. You have done nothing wrong, you have not spat in gods face, you have not deliberately gone out of your way to destroy the essence of real love, you were never shown what it was in the first place. Even if your mother was very attentive, alert, caring and present sooner or later you would have felt and sensed that you were expected to act a certain way, behave a certain way, mind your manners, be polite, listen and pay attention to what others were saying, do what is right, share your toys even if you don't want to , and why because that is what good boys and girls do, otherwise you are selfish and selfish people get left out and scolded.

Thus love has as far back as you can remember always had this expectation and agenda attached to it – thus leaving little room for you to experience just the joy of being yourself. The pure bliss of being alone in the backyard playing with siblings or friends or cousins without adults, in the sand pit, the mud, the long grass behind the shed, playing cops and robbers or cowboys and Indians, the joy and the bliss of just doing this, is closer to love, is what I am getting at, is what is real. Thus your focus for love has been on others, on having others with you, and doing things for you, when it should have been upon how you feel when you are with them, how you feel when you are playing, how you feel when you are jumping up and down dancing to Dad's Elvis or Beatle, or AC DC music. Just like the tree sways in the breeze to the music that only it and the breeze hears.

If you can learn to refocus your attention upon how you feel, the force of life which comes through you rather than what you are doing, what you are getting, who you are with, or who you are not with, you will make a very real and purposeful change within your life and being – one that can reveal to you what authentic love is. All this done easily and simply within your own home, working with me, no dusty meditation halls, no fasting, no no speaking, no incense, no hard floors, or hours of sitting, really what more could you ask for?

For you to have a much better sense of what authentic love feels like, the bliss it naturally evokes, the joy the happiness the pure force of awareness, cohesiveness and centredness it brings to your attention, you need to remember aspects of your childhood. To do this we will complete a simple and short exercise here and now so that you can at least get a glimpse of that which I am speaking. You may then re do the exercise later on tonight or sometime within the next day or two. So that you can broaden your understanding and appreciation of authentic love. Remembering always that real authentic love springs from bliss, this is its fertiliser, its soil, its home. If you are not experiencing bliss not even a slight joy or sense of balance, then what you are experiencing is not accurate and you will have to do the exercise again until you feel this bliss.

People's mind when they expect bliss, or know this is what the experience should entail at times let their minds create a fabricated sense of bliss, which is not so much a feeling but more an intellectual concept. Thus you must be weary of wolves in sheeps clothing, and be alert to the tricks your mind will or may play – remembering that how you are feeling, and feelings are centred in the heart centre will orientate you to where you need to be.

You should attempt this exercise in a light hearted manner, remember you are only after a glimpse, not an in depth spiritual experience, you just need a slight whiff of love to be able to more fully appreciate its dimension, feel and scope. This will obviously help you to be able to focus on seeing my version of love within your everyday, and will hopefully also help you to lighten your grip on your reality however slightly.

Childhood Reverie Contemplation

Close your eyes, relax and just soak back into yourself feeling good, put a smile on your face as you relax.

Just enjoy being away from your day, from the expectations of life for a moment or two.

Really sense how just smiling makes you feel, and bask in this nice light feeling.

Then when you are ready ask to go back to a time when you were young that also made you feel this way, all the while continuing just to soak back into this smile sensation.

Ensure that as you go back to a past memory that you are going back through the smile sensation, not leaving the smiley sensation, instead passing through it to the memory.

You may initially get a sense of happiness, laughter, running, you may see a childhood friend, or blurry hazy images may start to screen within your mind. Pay attention to what comes up, and follow all and everything back through the smiley sensation. Keeping it with you as you enter this domain.

Do not dismiss anything, and if nothing comes continue to focus on the smiley sensation and just bask in this for a time. You may just experience an overwhelming feeling of joy, happiness etc. Just allow what comes forward to come forward without too much analysing and assessing.

Just trust and follow what comes up here, you may stay here for as long or as little as you like.

When you are ready feel yourself coming back to your day, and slowly open both eyes.

Remain with the feeling this exercise has provoked for as long as you can. If some other feeling has arisen instead of joy or bliss, this is ok as well, this has surfaced for some good reason, trust that this has come up so that you are freer to experience a greater sense of bliss in the everyday.

This feeling will lead you to love, this feeling is at the core of love, if you persevere with my methods they will take you within to where an overwhelming sense of ecstasy pervades which would be like x by 100 the sensations you experienced within this exercise. Bliss is your home, your natural state of being, it overtakes and supersedes all other emotions – it will if you allow it to seek out all other emotions within you, overtake and dissolve them into its embrace and care. This is why Buddha's are laughing, why authentic gurus are unperturbed by that which happens around them, for this inner bliss pervades all and everything.

If you truly desire an authentic love, you must yearn to find this inner bliss which dwarfs all other feelings and emotions, all other circumstances, situations, people and places, objects and successes or failures. This bliss makes getting what you want in life outdated and unnecessary, it means that you can then easily accept that which comes or doesn't come. It means that you can allow others in your life to do what they feel they need to do to be happy without concern or worry for you know that they like you can at anytime tune into their inner bliss – which is not dependent on them being married, being straight, having children or a good job, having money or not. Even in absolute poverty can the riches of this inner bliss be gained.

The objects and things that money can buy cannot offer this inner bliss in any form or manner – they are empty, they are merely objects, they have no heart, they rarely open you to your own inner bliss – they are then valueless. When you can see and accept this beyond all else, when you can see that you hold your own key to happiness and bliss, then things begin to change within your mind and within your life. You suddenly start to see that you have ultimate power in your life, you have absolute wealth and control, you can choose bliss at any moment, and it is not a fabricated 'I'm gonna be positive' façade of happiness, it is an inner pool of happiness that simply exists for no reason at all. The more you walk this path with me the more you will see that indeed this bliss that you have just glimpsed at is encompassing and opens you naturally up to your multidimensionality.

Anything worthwhile must have worthwhile results, you must feel the effect and benefit of them, if not there would be little point continuing. Yet, you must also be willing to work to see these results, they will not simply fall into your lap. Learning to be receptive within the everyday, learning to just take a step back and stand within the space that naturally exists within you, is how you begin to work with this and accomplish this. This is not a race, it is not about how much you can do, in truth it is the opposite, it is how able you are to just let things go, to trust and allow and surrender. Because you have been trained by your society to do and become, you must now relearn its opposite, how not to be – not how to be lazy, not how to sleep, or become indifferent or uncaring – No this is not the point I am attempting to make. You must work earnestly in a concerted manner to stop yourself from doing too much but at the same time staying open to life, open to love, open to what comes up within you, what happens around you – this is an opening up, not a closing down – this is an opening which invigorates you, refreshes you, inspires you. You feel more alert, more aware, more in tune, you are naturally more compassionate, more flexible, more insightful, simply because you are choosing rather than get caught up in life and react immediately to it with your initial reaction, you are standing back and waiting and seeing what happens. This waiting, this standing back, this discipline to not rush in lulls you into a space whereby you just are – you just exist in the moment – you are not attempting to be mindful, you are not using effort or restraint, you are just waiting, you are just paying attention to what is happening within you rather than what is happening without, and this creates a spaciousness within you which is comforting, nourishing, calming and basks you in an unfamiliar energy which has the ability to still your mind, evoke breadth, depth and peace.

You are closer than you think, trust me beloved ones, your full potential awaits.

Mary xx

What is Love? Messages from Mary on Love and Fulfilment

Maya

Chapter Nine – Surrender

Beloveds rest assured that I am leading you to a place which is beyond your current perception of love, I am leading you to a place where you can access love regardless of whether you live amidst a bustling family life, are sharing a place with a few friends, or live alone. I am leading you to a place that exists within you, that you have total control over where and when you access it, it is not dependant on anyone being there, it is not dependant on how much you have, what job you are in, how many people look up to you and kiss your feet. My love just is – it is everywhere, it is in everything – you actually have to work pretty hard to cut yourselves off from it, but alas this is what your society has done and this is why you all suffer with so much stress.

It is hard work cramping your mind with thoughts when its natural state is to be open and fluid and spacious, you have to then cling to the thoughts that come, dwell on them continually, make small instances into large problems, so that more thoughts come, so that as you age there is less and less room in your mind for anything else, but this constant dominion of thought. You struggle with these hefty thoughts that wake you up in the middle of a peaceful dream, you face them head on in your car on your way to work when someone slows you down or cuts you off – everywhere you turn these thoughts are cramping into your mind, to make you feel sad and then happy and then numb and then sad and then happy and then numb.

You attempt to get away from this wall of thought by going on holiday, by seeking to enjoy the weekend, by getting drunk, by going out, by eating out, shopping etc. all these things you feel will help you to relax, will help you to brick by brick evaporate this wall of thought which constantly throws thoughts at you that you have made the wrong decision, things will go badly, you will fail, you will lose. In a bid to get away from these thoughts you become even more stressed, wired or aggravated, and thus as you speed up in a bid to get away from these thoughts, the thoughts themselves speed up.

You spend your day constantly pushing these thoughts aside and they then return with vengeance to menace you, to taunt you, to tease you and almost mock you. Yet as you have been unable to face them, to deal with them they appear luminous, authoritarian, real, ominous, and almost like God, their weight given greater credence by you, which again makes life tiresome, a burden, difficult and uncertain. Like being locked in a small room do these thought walls follow your every move and whether you are in a large city or on a sumptuous Caribbean island these thoughts remain. They may appear fainter for a time, they may seem more in the background as you are distracted by the scenery, but they are there, you still worry about work even when you are not there, you still worry about your family even when you are not with them, you still worry about your parents, your siblings, your money, your house and car even when you are miles and miles away.

By giving up projection you begin to take responsibility for these thoughts, you begin to see that what goes on in your inner world is emanating out into your outer world, and reflecting back to you. If you can persevere with this method if you can learn to depend upon it on a daily basis you will unravel the complexity of these thoughts within your mind, you will be able to diffuse and extinguish them much more easily and rapidly. As you are they continually catch you on the left foot, they creep up and surprise you at the oddest of moments, and you are defenceless against them purely because you are running from them, projecting them on to the outer world so that you can maintain and ascertain your supposed self.

While you continue in this manner will you be constantly heckled by the inner voice that must surface so that you can see all that lies within you. If you do not, if you refuse then age will bring with it a mid life crisis, you will reach a point where you simply cannot cope anymore, you will reach a point where your mind cannot cope anymore and it will suddenly just one day blank out on you, no matter how much fish oil you consume. Like all things your brain is prone to wear and tear, your mind is prone to wear and tear, and it will begin to break down either gradually and ever so slowly, or abruptly and suddenly. Working with projection is more effective and efficient than fish oil, more dependable than Sudoku, and longer lasting than memorising things.

When you begin to access frequencies and states of mind above your current level of awareness you actually relax the brain, and the mind, you begin to rejuvenate them, as the vibrations from higher planes of existence filtrate through the brain washing over it like a massage which cleans and purifies it. This is why meditation is so effective at keeping people looking younger and keeping their minds fresher, more alert, more conscious. When you access different frequencies available to the mind, they like allowing children to play in dirt, offer greater resistance to and immunity to hiccups and abnormalities which may cause damage if introduced early so that system can digest, acclimatise to and become more familiar with.

The best protection to anything is variety, the more sights, sounds, tastes, people, places and experiences you have the more broad will be your physiology and wellbeing. You make yourself stronger just by going to different places, by travelling to see different cultures, you open your eyes and your being to different concoctions of chemicals, different combinations of elements, all which diversify your own metabolism and make up.

When you can appreciate the inherent value in opening your mind up to new thoughts, new ideas, contemplation, introspection, pondering your life and what occurs within it, just sitting and looking abstractly at your life, you begin to create space or gaps through which higher energies can diffuse, and these energies help you to accept what you see, help you to accept your life, and appreciate it also. Isaac Newton one of you greatest minds has told you this *"I keep the subject constantly before me and wait 'til the first dawnings open slowly, by little and little, into a full and clear light."*

Albert Einstein another of your most revered minds used a method of picturing himself walking on a beam of light out into the Universe to assist him formulate his theories and ideas. So you can see that what I am talking about can and does have value, and the sad part is you are losing contact with this. You no longer have the time just to sit and be and think and ponder. You no longer have time just to sit in an orchard like Newton and speculate about why apples are not spinning as fast as the Earth does. You no longer have time just to appreciate where you are and write about the majestic panorama that you exist within like Wordsworth did. Instead you are logging in to Facebook to check what someone has said or done.

Your focus on the outer is overcoming you, is creeping into your previously held private times, and focussing your attention on the outer over and over, leaving your energetic being no time to rest and recuperate, to just be, to just sit and unwind. Let alone allow alternate thoughts to penetrate your mind, like Einstein and Newton did. Imagine if Newton can uncover and formulate a theory to prove gravity as well as the necessary mathematics to develop engines and machines, and Einstein can discover the aspects of the way in which gravity works, how the universe works, and Edison can invent the light bulb, what you could potentially discover and realise for yourself in your own life? Surely if these geniuses could make such world transforming discoveries, that you although not necessarily a genius, could uncover insights about your life, your being, your difficulties and problems? Surely if these men could make such landmark discoveries through the use of their own mind, that you could at least find ways to alleviate the stress and the trauma within your life?

Imagine what a difference this could make to your life? Imagine how much more optimistic and content you might feel if instead of just ignoring your difficulties or dodging them when they slap you in the face, you could penetrate into them, see them from a higher or broader perspective and then from there make acute decisions which could perhaps easily eradicate them from your life. Wouldn't this make contemplation worthwhile, wouldn't it make turning off the screen worth considering? Wouldn't you feel so much better about yourself and your life, and the control and power you have over it if you could accomplish this? Imagine how it would feel to not feel hopeless anymore, to not feel a victim, futile, at the mercy of a savage universe. Imagine once you did this once how much more motivated you would be to do it on a regular basis. You could potentially become an Einstein of your own making and world, you could look at your life, you could imagine aspects of it and from there theorise potential outcomes, possibilities, choices, alternatives. Imagine the power this would provide, imagine the sense of worthiness that would follow.

One of your most successful actors currently has often stated how his life has far exceeded all his expectations – yet while younger he continued to visualise his life and imagine the way he wanted it turn out. No one could deter him from doing this it seems, he committedly visualised his life as if on another level he understood the power of his own mind, his own intent. Look at the results. Yet here you sit a slave to the whims of those around you, unable and unsure, frightened and sceptical. Allowing what occurs in your life to thwart you, overcome you, dominate you, control you. You feel its weight bearing down on you as if you have no power, no say in what occurs or does not occur in your life. Instead you learn to escape from this reality, run from it even, by veg'ing out in front of the TV the Xbox, the computer. No wonder so many writers and futurists saw machines taking over the world, they are literally taking your power from you.

The only reason that you could possibly have for allowing this theft of your intelligence and integrity is that if you were not 100% aware that it even exists. The truth is you do not know that you have this power to reflect upon your life, to ask questions about what is happening within your world or your life – and you have not experienced the perception and insight that can be gathered from this process. Only when you have seen this firsthand can you see and know and believe in your own potency, intelligence and ability. As you are you are handicapped, incapacitated and alone – you have been severed from your power, from your reasoning capabilities and what is worse you do not even know that they are there, as you have been trained and taught only to revere information and facts from experts, from people outside of you, from doctors and lawyers, from scientists and mathematicians.

You do not realise that although you may not have received high grades at school that you still have the ability to extend your mind, to grow it, and to link it to your core, your centre, so that you can feel nourished and rejuvenated by your thinking processes, by your natural curiosity. Intelligence is not about memorising facts or information that other people have discovered, it is about thinking about how this information relates to you, is this information true for you, does it stand up? If not why not? If so, why?

Most of you use your mind at work to complete tasks for your employers and this is all, leaving the remainder of your mind unused, untouched, ignored. Like a dog that is tied up all the time, you never allow your mind to run free, to think about what could be, to contemplate where you are, who you are, what is important to you, what you don't want in your life, and what you do. You have simply lost touch with this naturally occurring process – you have swapped it for the screen, for conversation, for entertainment, for good food, and an array of trivialities that frequent your lives and world.

You have been doing this for so long now, that you are sculpting the new generation of children into vacuums that seek only to watch the screen – there is no substance - these children who are naturally creative, intelligent, curious, and filled with wonder about the world and where they live. Are being ushered into a world of plastic, and concrete and being inside all the time with no backyard, no forests, no greenery, no nights just sitting by the fire listening to stories from grandpa, or grandma, no real contact with this inner part of them which yearns to discover more and question and seek answers to. Instead they are being corralled into a way of life that cuts them off from this inner curiosity, this enthusiasm for life which brings with it great pleasure and sense of self.

Thus it makes sense that if you have been taught that intelligence is remembering isolated facts with no real context or understanding and appreciation for them, that you would fail to see the value in introspection and reverie. If you could just for a moment begin to feel how important this aspect of your life is, this aspect of sorting through the chaff in your mind, the thoughts, and opening up to them, creating space so that light may dawn on them, you may begin to glimpse at why your society is in the shape it is.

With all your experience as a society, with all the information that has been made available to you, with all the medical and scientific breakthroughs that have occurred and the psychological and social awareness that you have. Still you are no closer to knowing who you are, to knowing what you really need to survive in a manner which is palatable to you, which is in alignment to your values, and aims, and beliefs. For all your knowledge and information, for all the wars you have endured you are still no closer to ending them, to ending poverty, to correcting your lives so that you can benefit from these breakthroughs, these capabilities.

Instead you allow inertia, dysfunction and dissent to take over and rule your lives, your families, your towns, communities and countries, as you still to this day cannot grasp the very simple and understated necessity, of making time out to think to contemplate and revere that which surfaces from within you. Albert Einstein has told you "The *important thing is not to stop questioning. Curiosity has its own reason for existing. One cannot help but be in awe when he contemplates the mysteries of eternity, of life, of the marvellous structure of reality. It is enough if one tries merely to comprehend a little of this mystery every day. Never lose a holy curiosity."*

This can be applied even to contemplation of just your world and life, to seek to see the connection between your inner and outer world, what is happening in your life and how this connects to what is happening within you – for only through this will real and true understanding, appreciation and rejuvenation come. You can speak as much as you want about happiness, about tolerance, love, about finding purpose, these attributes will remain invisible to you unless you go within and find how they link and bond to you, your inner being, your inner world.

Your inner world may at first appear to be pure thought association and chaos, but this will change and temper as you persevere and sustain a habit of going within. When you adopt this art of seeking to go within you for answers, you open doors, wonderful doors, that allow light to penetrate, to excise mechanical thinking from your being, so that you can see the benefit of contemplation, of allowing thoughts to waft and dance in front of you, so that they can stream forward related thoughts, pictures, images which in many cases hold the answers to your difficulties and problems. Just as Descartes, Newton, and Einstein penetrated through the shield of superficial thoughts by questioning, contemplation and reverie so too can you learn to accentuate the thoughts that matter to you, and let these thoughts alone alight and take you on a journey of inner discovery and illumination.

This is where the mind and meditation meet, this is the axis whereby you begin to access your true intelligence, grandeur and potency. Until you have felt the fervour of this inner world, the aliveness, the broadness, scope and bliss are you blinded, impotent, manufactured and dull. Only by invigorating your life with this inner colour and realm and possibility do you then have a chance at revolutionising your world and the way in which all of you live.

I am Mary I come forward at this time in the hope that you will hear my words and sense my and my brother's love for you and concern. You may believe that there is no creator, there is only gravity, you may be sceptical that I can exist at all, or that I can communicate in this way, but I assure you, that regardless of how scanty, irrelevant or incorrect my words may appear that it is I who has brought them forward for your attention and consideration. I do so out of necessity and care, and hope that at least some of you may be able to put your ideals about me aside, so that you can stop judging whether or not I would say these things or not, as I can assure you, I am.

The closest experience you may have had to this inner reflection is while reading a very good book an author that you love, and you are reading something that seems to ignite something within you – you really agree with what the author is saying, you feel an affinity with the way in which he/she is saying it. They may be answering a question that you have had on your mind for a time – or revealing an answer to a problem or difficulty you are currently having. All of a sudden it's as if you have grown wings, you seem to be lifted up above yourself, somewhere inside it's as if an engine has started up, you feel an inner humming, a buzzing almost, your mind seems to be opening, stretching or has somehow become bigger. This sends you into an intense sense of bliss and awe, of things fitting together for once, of things gelling, making sense, and now you have this wonderful sense of content, warmth, largeness and scope.

This is the beginning of this inner process and world that I am attempting to describe and tempt you to visit. This inner orientation enables you to bring your experiences from life full circle back into your essence, your being, your mind which reflects the greater aspects of who you are. This creates a circuitry which enables energy to flow between you and your outer environment freely without restriction or obstacle. When this energy circulates between your life and your inner world, it frees up blockages, opens up your innate creativity, your inspiration, you're thinking capacities, your ability to understand others, your ability to offer a genuine love and compassion and real warmth. While this circuitry remains closed and unused, do you feel disassociated from where you are, out of synch, out of the loop, foreign, alien, and distraught at the meaningless and hopelessness that you see in the world. This will force you to close down to life even more, thus the attractiveness of the screen, in a bid to get away from this ever-present gnawing sensation that in truth there is nothing worth living for.

It is not your world you see, which is disappointing you, alienating you, confusing and annoying you – it is your inability to connect fully with it, and hook it into your inner world, your inner being which can help you see and appreciate the necessity and meaning within it. It has always been about you, never the earth or the world, or the people that you know and don't know – it's not about obtaining world peace, ending poverty and conflict – it's about you being able to look these aspects squarely in the face and ask **why?** When you can see the aspects of the world which you loathe and despise through your transformed vision and perception of your inner scientist, your inner philosopher, your inner master, you then understand and can comprehend for the first time in your life why they are there. When you can see and appreciate why they exist – then their multi-coloured aspects recede into the background. Whether they remain or go is of no consequence, for all along, as Einstein attempted to share – it is all relative – it is all up to you and how you perceive the world that matters, nothing else.

The wars, the violence, the indifference, the warlords, the drugs, the prostitution, and sex trade, paedophilia, and slave labour, the deforestation and the seeming crumbling of your environment comes back to you, it is all relative, it is all totally dependent on what you choose to see or don't choose to see. Only by making sense of the world, only by taking what you experience within and reflecting upon it, nourishing it, and staying with it like Newton did, till their aspects came out into a clear and full light, will you unlock the key to your dimension and life, and difficulty and pain.

While you continue to view all that you see in the world through your physical eyes, that are not connected to your inner world, your substance and potential, will you be hurled against the rocks time and time again for no good reason other than you simply do not know any better. Now is the time to see what you have been missing from your life and your consciousness for the entirety of your life, now is the time to feel the necessity of that which I am saying and to know that you must work with this idea if you stand any hope at transforming your world, your being and your life.

I have come forward to revolutionise your love on earth, but this is an impossibility if we do not first revolutionise your perception and orientation. You must overhaul the way you operate within the world if you want to access real love, true love, effective love. For love does exist, it is real, it is your natural state of being – but only when you have learnt how to open your inner circuitry can you experience and know it. You cannot just use words or sentences even to suggest that love exists here for all, for it simply does not, and will not reveal itself unless you are prepared to take the little that you appear to have and go within.

You may not be a genius, you are not going to discover calculus, gravity or velocity, you are not going to uncover a theory of relativity – but you alone are enough to begin to pierce through the happenings in your life, and not kill them with analysing and victimhood, but rather free them with the light of consciousness. Like letting butterflies out of a jar, watch the elements of your life dance before you, and through their associations, your questions, allow them to show you what lie hidden within and beyond them. Love requires this. You need to free yourself from the pain of your life, you need to stop believing in the pain and heartache which life constantly throws at you and anchor it within you, embrace it, love it, and let it reveal itself to you in its full dimension and capacity.

You are so busy running from it, numbing yourself so that you do not have to feel, to know, to care, that you cannot see that like a hidden cave it may appear just as a small crack or hole on the outside but once you get within it, it opens up into a magnificent, large and spacious room filled with the most precious crystals and gems. You have simply been too afraid to pierce through the outer façade, you have simple been led in the opposite direction, you have sat back and allowed the great thinkers of your world to dictate what should and should not occur on your earth. You have become complacent you have allowed authorities to dictate to you over and over again – without really appreciating your part and place within it all.

Now is the time to feel your place, and to know that even if no one knows what you are doing, or why you are doing it it does not matter, for you are doing it for yourself and your own development and evolution. Newton did not do any of his surmising and calculations for the benefit of others, for fame or notoriety, he had no intention of becoming well known, he did absolutely everything he did for himself, for the love of it, for the discovery, and the joy and animation that this provided him. He said at the end of his life that he had spent the entirety of his life like a boy on the seashore looking at and collecting shells, experimenting and playing, and yet the whole time the massive sea the ocean lay waiting undiscovered before him. He did it all because this is what he thrived on, without this his world was cold, empty and obtuse – and yet regardless of his intention or non-intention he remains one of your greatest mathematicians, one of your greatest thinkers and genius to this date. Learn from him, feel his wonder and curiosity of what lay all around him, and soak yourself in this – then take it within so that you too can be on the sea shore investigating what it is that really matters, really makes a difference.

If you can refocus your attention to your inner world, no matter how small or seemingly insignificant your first attempts might be, they will expand your perception and awareness of what is going on in your life. This inner world once nourished will begin to offer dreams, coincidences, people, books, experiences which all open your inner world up more so and make it a vital and real part of your life and existence. The more you begin to depend upon this method of going within, the more you trust it the greater will be its benefit and effect.

The only real requirement for this is making time alone, without distraction so that you can just be, settle back and allow what has been trapped within you from the day to surface and be seen by you in a relaxed fashion. The more you can relax into this process the more you will see and understand what surfaces. At the end of the day you have nothing to lose by trying this technique, at the end of the day the advantages for this far outweigh any negatives that your mind may attempt to sway you with. You must always be aware that the mind will attempt to sway you, deter you from any inner pursuit as it knows that through this you may gain the power to see above and beyond the mind and this is something it definitely does not want.

These simple ideas of going within are important- it may appear repetitive – but this is what you need. There is and can be only one way away from your earthly dilemmas and that is by going within. The inner world makes your life sane, it offers protection against heartache and disease, it enables you to grasp at a clear conscience which is not thwarted with guilt and shame at having more than others and not doing anything, or having less than others and not being ok with it.

Only by discovering your inner world can you realise what true equality is – and maintain it.

The path you seek is the path of devotion and surrender – the path of allowing a higher force to guide and protect you – I am this force. While you continue to think that you alone can control and manipulate your environment for your own good, while you believe that things will somehow work out ok, will you be left to a viscous cold world which does not care for you, as you do not care for yourself. Only when you can submit to a higher power can you invoke the power and the omnipotence the strength and the vision you require to lift you up and above your difficulties.

We are here, we will support you in your hour of need, we will elope and console you, but you must want us there, you must believe in us, sense us, feel us, and trust us. This is the path of devotion and surrender – handing over your whole being, your whole life, your whole perception to something which you know can see more than you. You are not doing this out of fear, out of guilt or shame or the desire to have your wishes granted, you are doing this purely as you have seen how devastating and debilitating your own choices have been – and how very out of synch with life and love and everything that is good they are. Only when you can see and feel wholeheartedly the ineffectiveness of your feeble mind, the maliciousness of it, the greed, the impurity, the weakness, and injustice, will you begin to realise that your only hope at salvation comes through surrender, trust and devotion.

I am not asking you to follow me blindly, I am not asking you to do anything that you do not wish to do – this is why I have been arguing with you, attempting to shed some light so that you can see that your little mind is prone to dysfunction and disease and cannot at this time and place be relied upon to help you move beyond your difficulties.

Any decision that your mind makes will attempt to lead you away from me, and my words and essence. It will do this as it wishes to remain in control, it wishes for you to be your own boss, by that it means that it wishes to control and boss you. For you are not your mind, you are actually far removed from it, you are separated from your mind, and it reflects who you are no more than a pond can reflect the brilliance and full breadth and scope of the moon at night. If you put your finger in the water you will see how transient this mind who has tricked you into believing that you are it, and it is you, is.

This is why devotion and humility, surrender and trust have been such an integral part of all major teachings. For by surrender you sink back away from the mind, the ego, you allow, you trust, you have faith. There can be no other way – you must relinquish your mind – you cannot do it your way when you are really only doing it the minds way. For you are not your mind and while you follow its hunches and dictates are you only repeating the past, as each and every day only triggers past memories, past emotion, past actions and behaviours. You will spend the rest of your life occupied with these notions, re hashing the past over and over again and learning nothing every time as a result, if you do not see and appreciate the wisdom in surrender.

You have nothing to lose, you have everything to gain – and only by trialling it will you begin to see and know the enormous benefits that await you if you do surrender – if you can hand control back to a force you know will not lead you astray with it.

To help you have a broader understanding of what I am attempting to convey I will include a text from Martin Luther 1483 -1546, titled 'Martin Luther's Definition of Faith' an excerpt from 'An Introduction to St. Paul's Letter to the Romans' Luther's German Bible of 1522 so that you have a broader understanding of what I am attempting to convey.

"Faith is not what some people think it is. Their human dream is a delusion. Because they observe that faith is not followed by good works or a better life, they fall into error, even though they speak and hear much about faith. 'Faith is not enough' they say, 'You must do good works, you must be pious to be saved.' They think that, when you hear the gospel, you start working, creating by your own strength a thankful heart which says, 'I believe.' That is what they think true faith is. But, because this is a human idea, a dream, the heart never learns anything from it, so it does nothing and reform doesn't come from this 'faith,' either."

"Instead, faith is God's work in us, that changes us and gives new birth from God. (John 1:13). It kills the Old Adam and makes us completely different people. It changes our hearts, our spirits, our thoughts and all our powers. It brings the Holy Spirit with it. Yes, it is a living, creative, active and powerful thing, this faith." ~ *" Faith is a living, bold trust in God's grace, so certain of God's favour that it would risk death a thousand times trusting in it. Such confidence*

and knowledge of God's grace makes you happy, joyful and bold in your relationship to God and all creatures. The Holy Spirit makes this happen through faith."

I don't think even I could say it better than this – this is the heart of all of your religions, your spiritual movements and ideals of perfection. Although you live in a material scientifically based age, does not mean that you are powerless or insignificant – although you have been taught to admire and admonish only experiment and factual observation, people's innate experiences and relationship with their God is just as real, is just as important as anything discovered about gravity or how the earth began, or whether or not climate change is actually occurring.

You have become on the whole a society of unbelievers, as you have misperceived what belief is, what faith is, as Martin Luther so aptly described in the above text – as you assume that faith is a blind willingness to submit to religious laws which may or may not be true – you question its pertinence its relevance in this modern age where people are encouraged to think for themselves, and discover truth for themselves. Yet, even so, you are not finding your own truth, you are simply getting lost in the plethora of information available to you, and until you can see that faith, surrender and trust are all about God's force working in you, and through you and with you, will you be unconsciously biased against this ancient method of release from burden through genuine surrender, and allowing God's grace to enter and fill you and be you.

Faith then is channelling higher energies receiving higher energies and accepting them into your being, more so than it is deciding to put your own interests and inclinations aside for the greater good. Faith then is about opening, it is about relaxing and letting go so that you can perceive and feel the bounty of goodness which elopes you through grace. This energy, Gods goodness, peace, love wholeness do not come because you deserve it, because you have earned it – No – they come as they themselves will transform you – there is nothing else required, nothing else you need do – the states of thought, of awareness that comes from allowing these energies, this force to pervade you cures all – offers you complete happiness and joyfulness as Martin puts it. Thus your religious institutions should not have placed so much emphasis on good works, original sin and repentance rather they should have shown you how God's grace works and heals in you, making you powerful, sinless, and holy. Only through accepting this premise will you find the freedom you seek from the pain of a life whereby you are enslaved to the notion that you have wronged and are simply unworthy.

Surrender then is not about sacrificing your own ideals and perceptions for the believed to be desire or law of God – or of being good and doing good works, surrender is about opening up and allowing the holy spirit, the essence of life to enter you, transform you and heal you. You are not relinquishing anything that you hold dear – you are not submitting to another being who appears to know how to take care of things better than you. You are not trying to induce a sense of humility or unworthiness in the face of a higher power, you are simply learning the art of relating to higher forces so that they can transform your vision to that which has greater clarity about the injustices of earth.

All too many of you – repeat the same worn out statements so that you can continue as you are the god of your own universe – you say 'if there is a God why does he allow this…… and this ……. to happen?' 'If there is a God why doesn't he show himself to us, so that there can be no doubt?' Yet, all the while he attempts to show you the perfection of your realm, the cohesion and benefit of it – but you turn from him, you run in fact in the opposite direction, as you have not learnt how to surrender, and when you are faced with his potent presence within you, you run scared as quick as you can back to your world of war, and drought and dis harmony. For although you dislike the events that may occur on earth, you dislike even more this presence which threatens to lift you up above your mind.

All of you have at some time in your life, come face to face with the essence of god, of the universe within you. You have sensed this force, this potency, this being, and you simply turned and walked the other way, it made you feel like you were going to go mad – you did not believe that such potency could exist within you – and you did not like the sense that this force would change the way you perceived and saw everything.

This force, the holy spirit, your higher self, or an angel energy was so penetrating that everything else that you held in your mind faded, became more obtuse, and irrelevant, and when you realised this, that it would literally take the world as you know it away from you, you quickly ran back in the opposite direction as quick as your little feet would carry you. You may have been a child when this occurred, it may have happened while you were grieving for a loved one, while you were amidst the grip of depression, when life betrayed you, let you down. Somewhere in your memory there is an instant and it may have been very brief but it is there, where you came into contact suddenly with something so potent, so overwhelming and effervescent that it immediately threatened your whole existence.

Thus, you are now left with the consequence of your choice, to live life severed from this aspect of who you are, that is you, and that loves you unconditionally. Doomed to a life of unlovableness, mood swings, trauma, and pain, simply because you did not want to submit or surrender to this force which threatened all you now believe to be true. While you need to hang onto your own perceptions about life, and while you need them to be real and necessary, the Holy Spirit, the force of life, God, Buddha whoever can do little indeed, for you alone are choosing your own reality moment to moment.

If you could allow yourself, however minutely, to surrender to whatever you find within yourself, whenever you give yourself the permission to slow down, relax and go within you will begin with time to taste again the potency of this force. But, you must know that it will again attempt to remove you from your mind, to lift you up to where you actually belong, and this is like a death – this is death, and if you are not prepared in any way for death, then so too are you not prepared for spiritual liberation, evolution and love. These aspects are all part of the same thing – and nothing but happiness, glee and rapture will you experience when you like Martin Luther allow yourself to be guided gently upwards to a place that offers clarity and understanding to all your misperceptions and dilemmas.

Surrender is crucial, surrender is the key – allowing a greater force to move within you, to slowly open you up to the magnificence and wonder of all that is – is the only cure, the only medicine, the only way to perceive and receive love and to then spontaneously without even your awareness be able to emanate it outwards for others. If you wish to revolutionise love on your earth, if you wish to embrace being loving, then so too must you grapple with the idea of surrender, and with death – for as weird and as uncomfortable as this may make you feel, it cannot be glimpsed at otherwise.

You are in my Heart Dear Ones – I come forward with my Brothers to lead you away from your crisis, dilemma and misinterpretations, I come forward to offer you substantial healing and a guaranteed correction of your perceptions so that love and wholeness, sanity and groundedness that connects you to where you are can be restored and sustained.

Chapter Ten – Allowing the Earth to Disintegrate.

Beloved Ones I am Mary,

The whole concept of Love to you is an attempt to make sense out of your life on earth, an attempt to make sense of life. To even out the scorecard, to make living worthwhile, for without people in your life who love you and need you, all becomes meaningless and futile. The wealth you may one day accumulate is worthless if you have no one to share it with – reaching your career goals empty if you cannot share it with someone tell someone. Buying that big house, going on holiday all becomes empty and hollow without people to savour them with.

Thus, love has become the glue that appears to make your life worth living, it offers you companionship and security, a friend to call on in your time of need, or your time of happiness. Thus, it is understandable that you do not like me pointing out the not so nice aspects of this love you have created, for as far as you are concerned this love is ok, it guarantees you a sense of comfort and companionship when all else falls down around you.

To be left totally alone on your earth, to be without companionship, to be without loved ones to talk to, call on, to gossip with, to share your disappointments and successes with seems almost like torture to you – this is what love is all about being there for each other. Yet, what you cannot see, what you do not see is how this sense of comfort that you have just being with loved ones, creates a type of swamp where you are prepared to put up with the injustices of life, you are prepared to settle just with what you have and believe in nothing else as this is what your home life supports and encourages.

It becomes very difficult to express yourself within your home environments if your innate impulses and urges go directly against the beliefs and values of other family members. This is what creates a lot of your conflict. Thus, to exist as a family unit, even if that is not a traditional nuclear family, even if that is just a group of your friends, co – workers, colleagues, mums from school, you all have to agree to a certain invisible bar that becomes the status quo. You search for what you have in common and you attempt to extend and improve upon this to enhance your relationships.

You then seek to ignore what is dissimilar, as you are aware that conflict ends relationships and will place undue pressure on the group as a whole, so differences are not often discussed or done so only minimally, in a bid to preserve and nurture your status quo, your invisible bar of agreeance, the level you are all comfortable communicating on. This is why people have secrets, this is why people feel ashamed or guilty, as they are constantly comparing themselves to the status quo. You all naturally will edit and change your style of conversation, the way in which you express yourself depending on who you are communicating with.

Although particularly in the immediate family environment you may be more comfortable with each other, and thus be able to express yourself more openly, still secrets will remain, as you attempt to uphold the status quo, your position within the group, your image. Conflict comes from expressing your unique ideas and viewpoints which are different to your loved ones – thus family life can be hectic at times, chaotic and all over the place, with most members retreating to their individual rooms in a bid to keep the peace.

This ideal of a family however, is secretly disabling you all, limiting your capacity, as it smothers you under the weight of having to get along. The inability to really express how you feel in each and every moment because you do not wish to create conflict, argue, or are forbidden to, has to have consequence. This consequence may be that you do not feel heard or listened to, it may make you feel abnormal, not good enough, or different, it may even create mistrust between you and your loved ones, you may even begin to resent them, hate them, ignore or detest them. Yet, more upsetting than even this is the fact that you are not encouraged to fully express yourself, and then you may never know the full potential or wisdom of what lies within you waiting.

While you constantly repress natural urges and remarks in a bid to sculpt yourself into the mould that your parents approve of, you understandably sever your innate connection to the stream of intelligence and insight that lies within you. As long as this remains you will feel stuck, out of the loop, repressed, annoyed, pissed and resentful towards your parents. But, it is not only the children who suffer the adults, the parents suffer also, as they are doing the same thing to themselves as they are their children, they are just better accustomed to it.

This is why when children finally leave the nest they experience a sense of independence and autonomy the likes of which they have ever known. Like having the roof taken off the house, suddenly there is all this open space, decisions to make, tasks to attend to, which may scare some unwittingly, and they may want again the security and familiarity of home life. Yet if the difficulties can be persevered with, a greater sense of being eventually comes forward, leaving the new adult wondering how they ever survived at home for so long. Generally people who have the courage to live alone and stay alone, have more insights into their life and being, than those who choose the even tempered family life.

Most of your greatest thinkers spent large portions of time alone – they may have married, they may not live alone, but within the framework of life they spent huge periods of time alone – as true intelligence is cultivated from this. When you are continually sacrificing your ideas, your desires, you're thinking processes for the family, when you are not allowed to discuss your inherent interests within the home, you begin to slowly lose contact with what enthrals and captivates you. As you lose contact with this, you lose contact with your true potential, you sacrifice it time and time again for the benefit of family. For the invisible bar of family life, of friends, and you stunt your growth, thus leaving you feeling numb, withered, bored, restless, and hopeless. Everything with time will become meaningless – as you yourself have cut yourself off from the inner child that wants to explore and invent and think about things that really matter to you.

This is why bringing back contemplation and time alone into your life is so very important and necessary – you need to reconnect with who you are on the inside – you need to feel again your wonder at the ants marching onwards without hesitation, you need to feel the awe you felt when you were small and you could spin and spin and spin then fall on the grass laughing and this was enough, this created absolute bliss and happiness for you. You need to be able to let go of what you think should be, you need to let go of what you think the world wants from you, and you need to be courageous enough and bold enough to do what you need to to achieve this.

Allowing the status quo of family life to unconsciously steer you down a path that may not be in your best interests – is not only heartbreaking, is not only sad for you and your inner health and wellbeing – it is sad for everyone, as they are doing it too. This has become your status quo, family has become your god, other people have become your god, and that being said you still treat each other abominably. You either fall into one of two categories, you do so much for your children and loved ones that you do not have a clue who you are, you run yourself ragged just trying to please others and prevent conflict, do what you perceive is necessary, alienating your soul and your instinct, your sense of goodness and purpose more and more each day – or you do the opposite you expect others to meet your requirements to feel loved, you have expectations which must be met – so that you can continue on your way without feeling disturbed or disrupted.

Either choice severs you from your true intelligence and instinct which lies dormant within you – you cannot see this currently as you have not seen what lies waiting for you within. Only when you have something to compare your current life against, only when you start to feel this intelligence and natural curiosity creeping forward can you appreciate what I am attempting to convey. The question then becomes 'Do you really want to live the rest of your life without tasting this intelligence that waits for you within?'

The more you choose each day to follow the status quo – to surrender your own inner urgings and desires for the society you have created, the more unhappy, dishevelled, bitter and depressed you will become. The more science and politics convinces you that there is nothing else only gravity, the more isolated and estranged you will become from your own nucleus, your own source of potency and power. Reason and religion go hand in hand, for religion is nothing more and nothing less than an offering of yourself to the essence of who you are – through devotion you recognise and esteem your connection to all that is, all that sustains and creates life. This may not be a man on a throne, a god as such, but it is a very real and significant force that interacts with you, supports and encourages you when you feel the most downtrodden and depleted. Science is nothing more than the search for how nature entwines with itself and creates the life as you know it. Science is an investigation a question seeking answers within the natural outer world and environment, religion also is a question….. who am I ? An inner investigation of your source and origin. Thus the two are quite compatible and complimentary, they should not be seen to oppose or negate each other.

The existence of one should not deny the existence of the other, to try and do this can only be an attempt to prioritise your preferred path over the other. Just as atoms, gravity and electrons can now be proven, so too can spiritual experience and devotion prove to the individual the existence of higher energies, the grace of god. Just because one involves experimentation with matter that all can observe does not make it more concrete or substantial than the monk who sits alone in his cave and chooses not to divulge the glory and ecstasy of his experiences. Why human experience and observation has become unsatisfactory or unsubstantial in your quest for understanding is puzzling – for surely how you interact with your environment and the world you live within has just as much impact upon it than your greatest inventions and discoveries……?

Revering the inner world of your psyche can be seen as no less of importance than understanding the physical components of the mind/brain…….can it? Who has taught you this way of living whereby everything that exists must be proven? Gamma and microwave rays did not exist before you had the tools and devices to detect them……….or did they? Just because you have not found a machine that can detect spirit that can detect God does not mean that he or it definitely does not exist does it? God is mysterious because this force changes depending upon the person who seeks him, who interacts with him, will differ in language skill, vocabulary, beliefs and desire to express this experience. You cannot doubt the experience of the Tibetan lamas and monks, the todgens anymore than you can doubt the existence of gravity, it may be invisible, but you can see the effects within the personality of the monks, the todgens, the masters, just as you can see the effect of gravity on objects, planets and us. The two do not oppose each other, they cannot, for they represent different aspects of the same thing. Albert Einstein wrote *"The whole of science is nothing more than a refinement of everyday thinking."* Much to the disbelief of the people around him. But what was he attempting to convey?

Perhaps he was alluding to the idea that there are no absolutes? Perhaps he was wanting people to see science as a continual progression towards gradually broader and broader understanding – rather than a small heavy fact that shuts out all other possibilities, perhaps he wanted students of science to feel the wonder, the opportunity, the discovery of science as something that opens people up to the diversity, complexity and majesty of the world you live within. Something which gradually grows and develops as your understanding of the cosmos and the world does.

Either side, religion or science does not have the right to impose itself upon the individual as an absolute, instead like Einstein and authentic spiritual masters, genuine authentic, individual and personal search should be encouraged and facilitated, in whatever direction the individual feels best with. On the outside it does not matter what it appears you are searching for, if you go within, if you seriously contemplate upon why you are here, why existence is here at all, you will begin to harness and utilise your inherent connection to these realms and whether that is science or religion does not matter – what matters is your sincerity, your determination to pierce through and beyond the status quo, so that you can find your original essence and from here all answers will come.

To do this, you must be able to let go of the world you see, you must be able to move beyond its parameters and aims, its limitations and beliefs, you must be able to penetrate life more effectively so that you can within contemplation make the discoveries and find the answers you seek. While you continue to work overtime, take the kids to 101 activities, please friends and siblings socialise and dream of expensive holidays and houses are you doomed to a life of hiding behind the screen, bored to tears but caught in a conundrum of not knowing a viable path out. Then as your life slowly slips and deteriorates right in front of your eyes, you become even more desperate, more alienated from who you are and more out of tune with your place in the universe and its place within you.

Now is the time to see that I have come to help you see above and beyond the trappings of your life and your world. You need this more than Africans need rain, water or money – you need this more than the environment needs your care and willingness to do what it takes to accomplish this, you need this more than your children need good inspirational caring teachers, you need this for without it all you have is empty and in vain. I come to take your hand to lead you away from your pain and difficulty, I come to show you a new way of interacting on earth, and of perceiving it – hold my hand and walk with me awhile, and see if you cannot slip into my shoes for a while and see what I can…….

While you continue to value only the physical and mental aspects of your lives are you bound to feel less than, incomplete, and miserable – you need a whole self philosophy if you are going to rise as a species above the mire of destruction and devastation that you are creating. The continual movement towards power, sex, money, drugs, war, and fame makes your species weaker than it should be. For you have quite some potent beings and systems available to you. Yet you squander and attempt to pull down anything of value on your planet, anyone trying to do the right thing on your planet is blacklisted, degraded and bombarded with mistruths and paranoia, all because forces and people who admonish power, greed and lust, cannot stand the ethical, the honest and the sincere among you.

This happens not only in world politics, between Muslims and Christians, between neighbouring countries, this happens not only within powerful multibillion companies, this happens not only every day at work, it happens in the home life, it happens between siblings, between fathers and sons, between mothers and daughters, the forces of dark and light interweave and dance, and fight just like children amongst all the distraction, the good food, and great conversation that you think you are having.

This balance of yin and yang, this play of forces is what facilitates and depletes you all at the same time. This is why you can be feeling on top of the world one moment and the next you are thrown into an abyss of uncontrollable anger, depression, meaninglessness. You have no ability to resist these forces your immunity to them is weak and almost non existent as you hand your power over to these forces daily, hourly, moment to moment.

This is why when you suddenly get outraged in your car when someone cuts you off, you have no control but to honk your horn, and put your hands up at them, this is why when you get home from work you are so exhausted you have to flop into a chair as quickly as possible as these forces have ravaged you, depleted you, they have been fighting within you all day, and now you are left feeling weak and powerless, restless and uptight. Until you can watch your thoughts, and observe the way in which you act and behave each day you will fail to see the pull and power that these forces have over you. Either force will have pros and cons for you, and you will inherently resonate to one of the forces more so than the other.

It may be difficult for you to understand how everything that you feel and think throughout the day, the ideas that you resonate with, your opinions about day to day topics, your reactions to what others do could be little more than a reflection of the stew of energy emanating from within you – but your inability to see it, or desire to see this does not alter its occurrence. All of you reduce to energy, all of you are made up of pieces from the sun, from the stars, from intergalactic explosions, from carbon and other elements created from these stellar blasts.

It is inconceivable to you also that you could be made mainly of carbon, to think that all your wonderful ideas, all your dreams and insights, and creative works could all be reduced to carbon is mind boggling to say the least – yet chemically this is true. But, this doesn't mean just because you are constructed with carbon that you are limited to it, obviously not – you far exceed the product of carbon as combined with other elements you create a metabolic physiology which seeks and thrives on diversity and expansion. The yin and yang of energetic force then, the interweaving of these energies give new life to the base elements within you creating a wonderful experiment of light versus dark.

You can then choose to each day resonate with thoughts that enforce the darkness, or the light, and this does not mean that one is preferential over the other, it simply means these forces represent different ends of the spectrum, both being required to enable diversity and elaboration. These forces can by some be considered myth, others fiction, others the natural rhythm of life – despite this all of you require the added impetus of these forces to sustain and maintain your equilibrium. Carbon alone, matter alone, neurons and synapses alone, cannot do this – the mystery of breeding life, cannot be fully explained until you accept and understand the interaction of energies upon your plane of existence.

Thus religion and myth provide stories which allude to the interaction of these energies and forces which although cannot be detected with your machines, explain much, the other side of the equation, the component that science as yet, cannot explain. Thus science and religion go hand in hand – they are two sides on the same continuum – ancient myths, tribal stories may seem quaint now, but the elements they express quite often reflect the effect of these energetic forces. The idea that natural disaster is some punishment from god extends well into your past, where tribal cultures believed these acts were a type of god simply because they had no other way of explaining them. Yet, their mechanism for dealing with these gods often showed a maturity and carefulness a considerateness which is lacking in your modern day era. Perhaps then learning to respect and admonish these natural processes, energies and forces is something you could all revisit in your attempts to understand Mother Nature and live in harmony with her.

When these two opposite poles of the continuum are brought into alignment, matter and energy a very funny thing occurs – both of them dissolve, they cease to exist, or they expand once mixed in exactly equal portions to create a different energy or a higher state of awareness. The interesting aspect to this is, matter and energy can only be aligned within individuals, within people, animals, plants, living organisms, only within this atmosphere can these two seemingly polar opposites unite and dissolve, and the dissolution is known to you as enlightenment.

Thus enlightenment is the cure to the affliction of these forces, of matter, whether you are suffering at the hand of life, or if these energetic forces are running rampant within you, enlightenment becomes the cure, it is and can be the only medicine. It doesn't matter what force created the universe, or what force sustains it, you will only penetrate beyond it through your inner world and vision. Only within can these forces align and create the beautiful majesty of evolution and transcendence. Just as everything outside of you is created with the same components that you are, so too everything inside of you, everything you experience within your inner world provides an energy which helps to assimilate and integrate those you find without. Everything is linked, and everything is leading you directly to the realisation that you need your inner world not only for a sense of peace, to get away from life for a while, but to literally align all the various energies you interact with daily, into a chemical concoction which sees you leaving the world, your mind, your illusions behind.

This is why there are so many stories of Indian, Tibetan, Chinese mystics and gurus being seen in two places at once, teleporting, disappearing, becoming invisible, defying the laws of gravity, of nature, as these laws no longer exist when you transcend them. When you are enlightened you have left the mind behind, the laws of nature no longer apply, this is why they can be seen by their disciples in London, at the same time they are seen in Delhi, or Chicago, this is why they can appear in dreams, and can know what they need to do in any given moment, even without using the mind. These masters appear before their disciples and devotees on a regular basis in vivid dreams that have quite a different quality to that of ordinary dreams, and can literally be seen walking off in the distance, or sitting nearby watching the devotee as a way of supporting the devotees inner search and path.

When everyday people like Jesus and Buddha experienced enlightenment they expressed it in very different terms – Jesus referred to it as the Kingdom of Heaven, his Fathers Kingdom as it represented a fullness to him, another world full of richness and wealth the likes of which the material world is unfamiliar with. Thus humanity interpreted this to mean the riches of gold and silver, and the idea that all worldly satisfactions would be thrust upon the seeker – freedom from pain and hunger and sadness and despair – thus only riches and perfection could attain this – and many Christians imagine themselves in heaven eating scrumptious meals, and drinking the best wine, listening to lovely music with not a care in the world. Yet, Jesus's life on earth was full of the opposite, his Kingdom was not dependent upon these riches, thus other Christians uphold a high moral or ethical code whereby these indulgences must be avoided or shunned as evil, as Jesus did not seek them or crave them.

The idea is neither to shun or to crave but to see beyond the lure of the world, and only the inner world can lead you there. The kingdom of heaven which is full, alludes to the fullness of being one experiences when the parameters of this life dissolve. When matter and energy fuse within you, you are literally lifted up above and away from the material world, planet earth, all the people you know, cars, roads, houses, the sun, the planets and stars all dissolve, they simply disappear. Instead you exist simply within this fullness, this energy, this source which supports and nourishes and uplifts every aspect of who you are within. Thus do you feel as if you have entered the kingdom of heaven, and although you are still on earth, still living in an earthly body, still without money, still having to go to work each day and face the laws of nature, you are somehow above and beyond it. Once you have witnessed it all falling away, it will never again tempt you with its rules, laws or dictates, it becomes redundant in a sense, and all that from therein matters, is this new land you found within where everything dissolves, and the kingdom, the fullness, is embraced and all pervading.

Buddha too was influential in his description of what he had found yet he described it in a totally different way to Jesus, he described it as an emptiness, a vastness, where absolutely nothing exists. This description may be slightly more accurate, but each individual is going to experience it according to their own being. Instead of a fullness that enriches him, Buddha termed it as an emptiness which saw everything disappear and become irrelevant. This vastness, consumed him, until such point that he ceased to exist, only emptiness remains – all illusion of the world simply drops away, all selfishness drops away, all desire drops away, all attachment drops away, everything just recedes and gives way to this nothingness, that occurs through pure relaxation into letting go.

Thus you can be in the world but not of it – you can have compassion for the people of earth who are amidst immense suffering and tribulation yet you are buoyed by this emptiness which clings to nothing not even compassion, not even virtue, not even good works, all is surrendered to, all falls away, only emptiness remains. Buddha's disciples like Jesus followers often sought to uphold the moral truths and became knotted up in this, rather than simply allowing the emptiness to pervade, as they could not quite grasp the necessary quotient of energy and matter to facilitate greater insight and penetration – but with time, if one perseveres it will and must come, your intent, your search brings it forth, invites it forward and this itself helps the right amounts of energy and matter fuse, so that the emptiness can pervade.

Two very different descriptions, for essentially the same experience – yet both these beings lived in different places in different times, and accordingly their language reflected the status quo of their time. All in a bid to penetrate devotees more convincingly so that they could discover that in essence this world does not exist. Essentially this is the teaching, this is the only way that their teachings make sense – you cannot uphold the world you now see and believe in, with all its troubles and disasters, corruption and injustices, entertainment, distractions and conversations and still seek and find the ultimate truth of your reality. It can be either or –

this world or that, the two cannot co-exist, you cannot sustain your allegiance to this world and be able to also juggle a new world that defies the laws and karma of this world. It would make the path even more arduous and harrowing. Thus their descriptions are accurate, and tempt the follower into trading in this world for another world, another state of existence, another plane of awareness.

This world, the world of your earthly life then, in the light of truth does not exist, it cannot, you must surrender completely to know truth. This is what makes enlightenment difficult, for you secretly do not wish to surrender your allegiance to what you have, you need to feel loved by those around you, you are attached to them, they are your source of love of goodness, you need them in your life, you need your coffee and movies and work, you need your spouses and cars and shoes, you need this life. You need this world, for the very idea that you might be alone in this vast universe or let alone in some isolating vastness overwhelms you with fear, anxiety and hesitation. You are running from it continually, your whole life is built around shielding yourself from the very idea that you are alone, that nothingness pervades, you are attempting to deny truth even though some of you proclaim that truth is what you seek. Even now while you are reading this you are attempting to deny or refute my statement, somewhere within you if you look now you will be disagreeing with, sceptical, unsure, and hesitant. For even the idea, not even a close experience or encounter, just the idea is enough to scare you, for this world is all you believe you have known, your memory seems to go back only within this life, if you go to a hypnotherapist you may find you go back to other lives, but still in this same world, a different time, yes, but this same world.

Thus all your memories, your experiences, your emotions, your beliefs, your morals, and ethics, your relationships are all based in this material world, where fact and science are admonished, and where religion also only forces you to do good works and focus on the outer, not on the inner world, the inner experience the inner planes of existence. Only when you have had enough experience with these inner planes of existence, only when you have persevered with meditation, relaxation, contemplation, going within, reverie, just letting go, just being in nature, will you even slightly begin to sense these other planes of existence. Only when you feel and sense these, only when you relax into them and allow their energy to descend into you and mingle with your matter, will you have courage enough to defy the laws of your mind, and let go of the illusion of this world.

For my friends this is what your world is – sun or no sun, gravity or no gravity, carbon or no carbon, cars or no cars, oceans or no oceans, trees or no trees this is what your world is – it is nothing more and nothing less than a hologram – an intricate maze or puzzle sculpted around you and your beliefs – it likes Einstein's theory of relativity bends around you, to provide you with enough seeming evidence that earth exists, but in the light of day there is and can be only the source from which all of us have come. Why would this energetic source expend huge amounts of energy and resource to create a material universe, that is dense and weighty and needy, when it can just as easily create a hologram that makes you think you are living on planet earth, and makes it appear real and substantial, so that you can have the experiences you desire without wasting huge amounts of resource and elaborate construction and energy.

I know this is hard for you to hear, I know particularly as you are constantly running from truth it becomes even more difficult to accept it – but when you go within, when you let go, when you become enlightened, you will see how impermanent and unreal this world and universe actually are. Just as your thoughts that at one time can appear so real and significant to you, and you may even believe they are you, or God, can dissipate and dissolve as quickly from whence they came, so too your body, your mind, your world can dissolve and disappear easily and effortlessly.

All meditators even beginning meditators have had the experience of staring at their hand or an object only to see it start to move, become larger, move or ripple in unnatural ways and finally disappear. Meditators have seen themselves disappear in mirrors, have seen the walls of their homes disappear, have left their bodies and are suddenly flying out in the middle of empty space. Even non meditators have had out of body experiences, have seen spirits, have heard rumours about the existence of other realities besides this one. Yet you all deny this, you all run from it, you refuse to look into it, not because you do not have the time, you simply don't believe it could be real, and you don't want to believe it is possible either. To think that you can leave this world totally behind through simply walking up the stairs within your mind, and letting yourself fall into the unknown is devastatingly too close to home, and that is scary. For just like death, you then have to wonder 'What will happen to me – where will I go?' Afraid that what you will lose will be more substantial than what you will gain.

Of course you want your world to be real, of course you want it to be the only world, just like in Copernicus times you want everything that exists to revolve around earth, around your perception of what is. When you suddenly then encounter information, experiences or people that negate this, then of course you will shun it, run from it, distract yourself from it, for you have invested far too much in this world and life, far too much to see it disintegrate and become meaningless right before your eyes.

If suddenly this world loses its significance even, not so much even its validity, you become frightened, like the Christians and Catholics became when evidence arose that the earth was indeed much older than was stated in the bible, and that indeed you evolved from apes rather than instantaneously manifesting as assumed in the bible. Thus forcing them to find a broader philosophy that incorporated these new findings so that their churches did not lose relevance or allegiance from its members. So too, hearing my words scares you I may not be pointing out scientific experimentation or fact that proves this theory, but you only have to look into outer space through a telescope to realise that indeed your world will one day be caught up in an explosion beyond measure, and that will obviously be the final end.

Anything that is not permanent, is not everlasting cannot be real, you could say it was only a dream. Just like your ancient civilisations that have all been wiped out – their existence seems not to matter. You may guess and conclude theories about how they lived and perished, and what implications this has for you, but this is just speculation and overall, although interesting, they are gone, they like a fleeting dream have been and gone, just as your species will come and go also. You cannot deceive yourself from this fact – your society may survive another 20 years or another 2000 or even 2000000, but it will end, running from this – ignoring this idea that everything that you do here in your everyday life is not going to matter that much in the grander scheme of things can be hard to accept, but nonetheless true.

This does not make your lives meaningless, but certainly it should help you to see and to feel that in the end if you are going to die, if your civilisation is going to be erased, if future generations or civilisations are going to know very little about the way you lived, and what you did or didn't do, wouldn't it be good to at least then let yourself live the way you want to live, rather than being dominated by the invisible status quo which will simply cease to exist one day.

In the same way that this argument is compelling when you truly contemplate your impermanency, so too is the argument that this reality does not even exist at all. When you have experienced or glimpsed at another reality through meditation, crisis, or some inner realisation, rather than running from it and attempting to forget it even happened, you yourself are going to be far better off, looking into this and seeking to discover its meaning for you. Surely being able to see beyond the constraints and limitation of this world, helps you to rise above it, helps you to also rise above the restriction and compulsion of beliefs and conditioning within your mind.

Your mind is operating in direct alignment to the dictates of this reality or world – your conditioning, your childhood experiences, what you were taught at school and Sunday school, in your neighbourhood all dominate the power of the constraints within your mind. It is difficult for you then to accept or see above and beyond them, thus the broad appeal of hallucinogenic – drugs, alcohol as these substances loosen the grip of reality, and help you align to a broader perception that is not caged in by your conditioning.

Ancient tribes, the Maya, the native Indians of the Americas all smoked or consumed potent herbs which evoked altered states of awareness, so that greater insight may be given into certain circumstances, or communication with deceased elders or spirits may occur. Even today many cultures, many elders consume potent concoctions of herbs for this purpose. It loosens the grip on this reality, and helps them see beyond the limitation that you as a species have imposed upon yourselves. Only when you have experienced this firsthand and have experimented with it in such a way that you can gain substantial insight and benefit from it, can you see the limitations that have automatically been imposed within your mind.

When you can even no matter how slightly begin to appreciate that there could be more much more out there than your current understanding, suddenly the world opens up before you like a Pandora's box and you are free to think about things that previously would not even occur to you. When you can see or sense the relativity that all of you live within, when you can appreciate how not only the universe bends to your perception but the whole world, you begin to uncover the power and majesty of your own perception and insight. Accepting that this world is not real, is the only theory that can set you free from it – it doesn't make you weird or out there, or a fruit loop, Einstein, Newton, Kepler, Emerson, Buddha and Cayce these are the people who you are joining among countless Indian chiefs, tribal elders, all who found the link the bridge between the inner world and the outer one, a link which offers far greater insight into the workings of your world, if not its impermanency. If you can challenge and question the thoughts and beliefs within your mind, you begin to uncover a doorway within your mind that leads directly to a place of depth, substance and richness within you – this is where genius springs from, this is where your freedom, release and liberation awaits.

This place is sacred not only for the insight it offers, but the overall sense of understanding and cohesion it provides – it helps you to make sense of the bigger picture – it helps you to see and to know your place in the world, rather than feeling out of the loop, rather than feeling disconnected and alienated from your world and all that occurs within it, suddenly you feel central and integral to what is happening you feel understood as you grapple with the perfection of how this life, your world and your consciousness all fit together. There can be no greater ahha moment than this, there can be no greater sense of peace and alignment and freedom than what this provides. All of you have access to it, but you are heading directly in the opposite direction to it daily – you shun it, like a trap door that leads down to your basement after you have walked over it many times you forget it's there, you buy a rug cover it, and then you easily learn to focus only on the furniture in your room, rather than wondering about what has happened to the goods stored in the basement.

You have walked over your inner door to freedom so often that when I now try and tell you that your world does not exist you think I am misleading you, or worse fooling myself or trying to fool you. The colour of your life, the complexity of work life, of getting on with co-workers, of going out, and watching TV, of managing the kids and housework, and keeping track of what your husbands are doing, your friends and siblings and parents, all like furniture in the room has distracted you away from that lifeline that will and can save you from your own illusions and delusions – only when you are game enough to tap back into this lifeline – only when you are game enough to remove the rug on the floor, look at the trap door and perhaps even pry it open a little will you begin to see and to know that indeed there is more to this reality than what you currently can see or sense.

I will continue with this concept in the following chapter offering you exercises to help you rediscover the trap door.........

You are in my heart beloveds, I come forward with my and your brothers to show you how to get the most out of your world and life. I come to free you from the self-imposed prison you have allowed to dominate you since your early years. I have come to show you that there is a way for you to reinvigorate your life and search and being, rather than continually trying to ignore the boredom and restlessness that all of you live with through addiction and compulsion. I show you the real way to live on earth, a way which is not about just fulfilling dreams or thoughts that come from insecurity and fear – I come to lead you through the woods of your mind to the hidden oasis of life force, insight, penetration and cohesion. Then it does not matter if you are a movie star, an office worker, or a stay at home mum, for each and every one of you has access to the medicine that will and can provide not only greater immunity to the despair of life, but greater understanding and purpose within it........

What is Love? Messages from Mary on Love and Fulfilment

Maya

Chapter Eleven – Opening up to your inner Oasis.

Beloved Ones the choice is yours continue as you are, never really knowing the full potential of who you are, never experiencing the depth and the groundedness that comes just from being in contact with your multidimensionality, or dare to challenge the beliefs and values that you uphold and have been reared with. Hold my hands dear ones and feel me there beside you encouraging you to walk with me, to see things in a different light, to know the world through your inner eyes, your eyes of perception and awareness.

All too often you have made rushed decisions in your life, decisions which come from fear, from a sense of need rather than a sense of purpose or becoming all you can be. All too often you have allowed other people in your life, and their immature demands to rule and dictate to you, your path and aim. You are too easily influenced, too easily swayed by the status quo, of being good, of what you think is the right thing to do, regardless of how it impacts the inner you – the you who you really are. Forcing you to smother time and time again the inner urgings and feelings which seek your release and freedom from this bondage, from this restriction which have you believing that you are 5 senses nothing else and nothing more.

While you continue in this manner, while you allow this pattern of behaviour to be you, to represent you you lose something vital and important, you lose contact with who you are, you lose your ability to receive and absorb love and peace, goodness, content and happiness. Everything to which you and your society esteems you lose because you have not been brave enough to see what lies beyond the top of the hill, you have not been genuine enough in your search to see what substance creates and sustains you. You have not wanted to forsake your distractions, your entertainments, your screens, good conversation and coffee for the irrepressible allure of immense connectedness you will feel when you discover your soul, your direct link to the cosmos, to me, to the universe and to all that is. While you continue in this manner what is it that you think you will achieve – a promotion, more money, freedom from mortgage repayments, to be revered amongst friends and family who themselves are so cut off from who they are that they can in earnest not appreciate you or even see you. For they like you are full of the past, of things they must do, never-ending lists, and plans and ideas, which will in the end prove futile at gaining you love and care.

If you could only glimpse my perspective of your life, only for a moment, you would immediately sense the confusion and fear that is smothering you moment to moment – you are just so accustomed to it now that you do not even see it or know it is there. Like oxygen you take it for granted you no longer even realise it is there – but I can assure you my beloveds each and every choice you are making on a daily basis is coming from fear rather than love. To correct this, to be able to feel loved and valued and whole, you will need to start waiting more when a decision needs to be made even a small one – and seeing if there are other choices that you have not considered before jumping in head first to a choice of fear and all the consequences that this will entail.

Just as when your children nag you enough you normally give in as you cannot take their incessant whinging anymore, so too are the majority of choices that you are making dictated to by this ever-present force called fear. When you are not alert, when you do not take the necessary time required for honest reflection and consideration of your options, you will automatically fall into fear. There is no doubt, fear is the path you are on, it takes courage to rise above fear just to even see that other possibilities do exist. Normally you are surrounded by 3 fearful choices to 1 choice that promotes love, thus even if you are contemplating two possibilities both of these most likely come from fear. To access love, to access your inner being, to access a greater awareness and choice you need to penetrate deep within you, sometimes dreams will assist, coincidences, signs, are all significant aspects of what I am speaking about – and certain people when faced with life changing decisions have had at one time or other – experienced these phenomena which helped them make an out of the ordinary decision which directly affected and influenced their life path.

Thus what I am attempting to convey is not an impossibility, but a skill like all things needs to be learnt and practised if it is to become a part of your life, and your consciousness. Once you have learnt this skill, once you can begin to stop and take stock of what is happening within your life, and where you are, taking a step back to see the bigger picture – you will see how effortless, easy and comforting this decision making process actually is. It invigorates you, the process itself makes you feel alive, connected and unified more so within your life. And more often than not, these choices immediately have benefits for you, in that less difficulty, hardship and complexity is evoked.

As you continue to make decisions in this way, you invite an energy into your life, which relaxes into life and trusts life, rather than fighting with it or resisting it – this incites confidence and willingness to be open and accepting of life, rather than shutting down to it and fearing it, running from it, avoiding it. This will naturally and effortlessly cure addictions and compulsions with time, and if not eradicate them, at least take the edge off them, reduce their influence and pull, and give the individual much more breathing space to see around the edges of this addiction or compulsion.

The difficulties in your life, within your own being, whether you are anxious, moody or prone to depression on certain days or in certain circumstances, the difficulties within your family, within your community of friends, within your town or city, your country or even globally can all be sourced back to you and choices you are making. If you learn how to choose love over fear, if you learn how to stay open and trusting of life, then this will automatically ripple out and affect the people in your life, and world. You need do nothing. Hear me again – you need to nothing. The energy itself which you emanate is the most potent transformational force, the most adept healer, the wisest counsellor, the absolute best role model – this energy, like the holy trinity – the holy spirit – weaves its way through and around you and your life so convincingly and adeptly, that any attempt by you to teach or preach or change others looks meek and weak and absurd in comparison.

This is where the heart of transformation lies, it lies in love, in the energy which is at your source and the source of everything else. It lies in your ability to be open and receptive and trusting of what life offers you – and allowing that to lead and guide you, rather than allowing the head the mind to intervene with all its plans for success, power and glory. It is not that hard to differentiate between love and fear, for if you look closer at them a decision coming from fear is attempting to avoid something, and a decision coming from love is opening to something rather than recoiling. It may take time to penetrate through to where each choice is coming from but once you do, it will become crystal clear – fear is definitely avoidance – you will be worried and concerned, that if you do not do this then something uncomfortable may occur. Love will be the opposite, you will be embracing this eternal trust and confidence that the universe has your best interests at heart, thus there is no need to make a rushed panicked decision, there is plenty of time, and you feel no fear either way that something ill-conceived may occur. You take your focus off of expectation and desire, and place it firmly on trust and the willingness to accept that what comes your way is for your learning and betterment.

When you take time to contemplate what is happening in your life, when you penetrate inside your being to a place that is less influenced by the outer world, you begin to sense a totally new way of seeing what is occurring in your life, and suddenly things start to make sense and choices become easier to make, with much less dread attached to them. As opposed to your normal way of dealing with life, which is to avoid looking at your difficulties, and refuse to make choices and decisions surrounding them until such time that disaster strikes and it is taken out of your hands. This pattern of avoidance creates much havoc and strife in your life – which closes you down even more so to life and living and the people you find within it.

Thus choosing love, taking time to contemplate your life, so that you can see more clearly where your difficulties arise – and responding with love, and trust and willingness to see how this all fits together – begins to reverse the feeling of fear and dread that has entered your life and being. This is going to take time to get the hang of – this is going to require some skill, patience and kindness towards yourself on your part – but the end result will be very worthwhile – I can assure you.

Too often you are making last minute rushed decisions as you continue to avoid difficulty – and this normally exacerbates your troubles – to choose love, to start to reverse this dynamic all you need do is intervene earlier, through practicing being alone each day, contemplating each day, going over each day what has happened within your life, and how you feel about what is going on, how your loved ones feel, what is really happening within them, see if you cannot penetrate into them further by going further within yourself – and you may be surprised by how much you actually learn from this pursuit.

If you begin to appreciate that love is your source and is the source of everything, and is a form of energy you can begin to see how problems can be resolved simply by going within you, looking at what is happening and addressing the problem there rather than constantly bickering with loved ones on the outside. Rather than exhausting yourself running after others in an attempt to please them, go within and reconcile the difficulty there, and you may be pleasantly surprised that this also impacts and has real effect within your life and being.

If you can accept that you are creating every aspect of your life from the thoughts and emotions and feelings that you hold within, you can begin to appreciate and sense that acknowledging these thoughts and emotions, and being able to stay with them rather than running from them, corrects imbalances that may occur due to avoidance. When you free your being from these heavy thoughts, when you face these emotions head on, and allow them to be, when you penetrate through to the other side of them, suddenly the weight and power that they seemed to have in your life dissipates and dissolves.

Like a chemical imbalance in your brain – looking at these emotions and thoughts, and more than this just being still, just allowing the holy spirit of life and love to be with you in certain moments, has a magical power that uplifts you – and more effectively than rigorous exercise or fish oil, literally changes the chemicals in your brain, creating a space through which you can perceive your whole life in a different manner. This is a crucial ingredient to your health, wellbeing and longevity, just as exercise is important, just as eating vitamin rich foods is important, just as love and feeling loved is important, just as being able to communicate efficiently is important, so too is time alone, time for inner reflection and contemplation and meditation. This is something your screen dominated society is losing and is losing fast – and you have to stop and ask yourselves is this really the way you want to rear your future generations, with such high dependence and affinity with the screen, that to be without one is debilitating and destabilising for them?

Currently you are not aware of that which I am speaking, so the value of what I am saying to you is reduced – only those brave souls who have ventured within can grasp the importance of what I am saying. But if you give yourself some time to experiment, you will see that indeed everything that I allude to is true and correct. There is a wealth of vitality waiting within you, a magical sanctuary which languishes with the Holy Spirit, with the spiritual ancestors of the past, and receives intuitive insight and information from them.

Within you all is a deep and unwavering connection to the whole universe. You do not need space ships, or rockets to get you there, you can be there instantly, if only you are brave enough to go within in a concerted and earnest manner.

It will not happen overnight, you will not experience the vastness of which you are immediately, for that humility, sincerity and patience is required – that is just the way of things – just as it would be useless for a Spanish speaking person to go to a beginners physics class in English, so too is it useless for you to go within without evoking humility, patience and reverence – for to understand the realm which you will enter when you go within you need these qualities – they like an interpreter help you to understand and accept the eloquence, beauty and magic of the place you have found, your inner oasis.

Just because you have lived the majority of your life without seemingly experiencing your inner oasis, does not mean that it does not exist, it does not mean that it is horse play, nonsense or pure speculation or imagination – it simply means anyone who discounts it has not found it – it's as simple as that. Somewhere in your being you can feel and know it does exist, somewhere within you you know life does not really make any sense without it. Somewhere in your being you sense your innate connection to the cosmos, it's just the role models for this have been so few, so seemingly far away, they may have lived in another culture, another era, another state of awareness.

Even people who stand before a Buddha a master have trouble understanding what the Buddha or master is talking about, as they have no reference point. There can be none until you go within and find the place from which all masters spring from – your mind cannot appreciate the no mind, the unenlightened cannot appreciate the enlightened, not really, not until you go within to your core and experience even only a glimpse, the slightest glimpse is enough, and it helps many sadhus, many disciples to see and understand and know the truth, beauty and authenticity or their particular master or Buddha. Without this glimpse, without going within sannyasins, students may be tricked into thinking that it was too far-fetched, that years after it does not bear any relevance to the modern world, to the way in which you live – but these opinions can only come from those who did not get their own personal glimpse. Normally if you are with a master, if that master cherishes you, you will get that glimpse, they can themselves concoct the energy necessary for the students benefit, for that ever so precious glimpse. If you have studied or worked with a sincere authentic master, with no glimpse of the beyond, of your inner sanctuary, then I can only assume the time has not yet come, you are not yet ready to receive, or you are incapable of seeing.

The energy itself is the ultimate dictator, the master himself a slave to it – the master cannot go against the patterns, cycle, will of the energy - and it will only come where it is invited, where it is welcomed, it will not come to those who doubt, who are sceptical, it will not come to those who are unconvinced. Somewhere within you, through gallantly moving forward within, you will stumble across the link, the bridge, that enables you to see what I am speaking about, enables you to feel and to become aware of your inner connection to everything – then a glimpse becomes possible, then slowly gradually more and more glimpses will come, until such time that they start blurring your vision with the truth of reality, and with the impermanence of yours.

This process is sacred, and it entails total surrender on your part, total openness and willingness to let go of everything in this world that you hold dear. This is why the experts of life will taunt you, and call it fantasy, imagination and speculation, it cannot be proven, for they do not want it proven – they want only the world that they perceive and have invested themselves in. Letting go of what you perceive you have is the most difficult thing in the world for you to do – but only through doing it are you free from it. Monks who tell you that you can hold the world in one hand and dharma in the other are tricking you – there is no middle ground – there can only be the choice between love and fear. Love cannot exist in this world if you cannot let go of the world, and once you can let go of this world and everything that you cherish within it, there is simply no need to speak about a balanced path of attaining dharma lassoing it and bringing it down into the earth. This is just as imaginary as the fear that now exists or seems to exist on your earth.

When you become enlightened, there is no good and bad, there is no love or fear, there is no our world or your world – you simply exist, there are no concepts, no boundaries that need to be reinforced, no need for balance, no need for groundedness, no need to stop yourself floating off, no need to be here in the body or not here in the body, everything stops. You have this old saying 'before enlightenment chop wood, carry water. After enlightenment chop wood, carry water.' Yet even this has been misinterpreted by the masses, not everyone but certainly the masses – yes you still live the same life, after enlightenment, a space ship does not come and pick you up and take you somewhere else, there is no need, where you are is transformed, you see things as they really are, but are unable to remember it. All concepts cease, all ideas cease – they may still float through your being, but they like leaves in a stream have no impact or weight.

So after enlightenment, it still appears as if you are chopping wood and carrying water, so on the outer it appears as if nothing much has changed, yet much has transformed within you – so the second part of the saying should end with ' After enlightenment the axe chops wood, the bucket carries water.' For there is no one else there, nothing else is there, you do not exist, your thoughts do not exist, your dreams do not exist, the person who you were before enlightenment no longer exists – thus dharma does not exist, ignorance does not exist, problems do not exist, enlightenment does not exist. You simply are – without good reason or an articulated explanation – you just are…….

There can be then, no intellectual concept about achieving nirvana while still in the world, you must rescind and relinquish this world in its totality – there are no halves, no crossroads, it is all or nothing. This in itself is a concept that does not exist or matter after enlightenment – but this concept will assist you to reach this bridge within you, where a glimpse becomes possible. Nothing, absolutely nothing in this world or any other can prepare you for this glimpse, you will never forget it, and it will happen when you least expect it, and it will come in a way that shocks and contradicts all your current beliefs and theories.

I have come to let you know that this is real and true, and regardless of what your politicians and scientists, and philosophers or psychologists would have you believe, this glimpse, this state of awareness, which is actually your natural state, your homeostasis, is there for you waiting to be discovered. It appears the fog of life, is suffocating you all, smothering you with this perception that you can only be who and what your outer life reflects back to you, you can only be what other people believe you are, you can only be what you have done in your life, what you have achieved, what you have meant to others, what footprints you leave behind. This is not so, this is pure speculation and nonsense as far as I am concerned, for you exist regardless, and who you are is inextinguishable, effervescent, and an integral component of everything else – you are everywhere and in everything. Just as carbon inhabits your body, and constructs much of the matter in your world, so too are you in everything and everywhere, there is nothing to prove, nothing to do, just accept that right now in this moment here with me, can you remove the curtain and see, sense and feel something much mightier and convincing than anything that could exist outside of who you are. Here with me, with your defences down, you can feel a small pendulum weighted taking you inside to your core....... To your hara, your solar plexus, this inner door way will reveal the truth, the inescapable truth that things are not what they seem .... and only through forsaking what you think you know, will you find the truth of what is...........

Being in this world seems to pose many problems for spiritualists – you seem to want to find a way to be in the world at the same time as you are attempting to transcend it. This is not an option, although you can with much concerted effort, patience and forbearance find a path that enables you to eventually bring the energies harnessed through liberation down into the physical – the very minute percentage of the population who would be able to successfully do this permanently is so small that it would be on the whole misleading to speak about it. I am wanting you the everyday person to be able to move beyond your mind, and I can only help you do this, I can only help you embrace love, if you can see and accept the necessity of finding this bridge within you.

Until such time that you find this bridge – you cannot understand in truth my perception of love – until you find this bridge – love will continue to be an invisible concept that merely shows itself when you are alone and missing having people with you – or when you are on a high for the things in your life are going according to plan. It will never become a permanent, real and tangible factor in your life, instead like a car that is just over the hill you may see its headlights, or hear its engine, but you will not and cannot see the real and effective gifts that it can shower upon you, over and over and over again.

Going within is how you then access love, going within is how you learn to feel, see and receive love and therefore also offer it to others. While you continue in your little bubble of need, of having to please will love evade you time and time again. Only when you have the courage to go within, to feel what's there, to see what's there will you know what true authentic love and bliss are ....

Maya

Chapter Twelve – Incorporating Love into your Everyday.

Love is receptivity – Beloved Ones please remember this – if you are seeking love, if you are seeking to feel loved, to feel whole and at peace you must allow yourself to be open and receptive to everything that comes to you. Currently you cut yourself off from life, through continually planning and daydreaming about what you would like to occur. You then have little everyday disappointments and altercations when things don't go as well as you had hoped. You then react to what is happening in your life, the upsets and disappointments and many of you can spend your whole day reacting to something you did not like or expect, rather than soaking in what goodness and joy the day will naturally and effortlessly bring forward.

This is a lifestyle choice a way of perceiving your life which is in a let go attitude, which stands back and trusts life, rather than superimposing your rather limited and shallow wants and plans onto the day. The more you can just allow your plans and daydreams to travel through your mind, like a miniature train and leave undisturbed the better off you will be. If something does not work out, rather than feeling disappointed try and focus on opening up and just being there in the day and wait and see what life brings forward for you. Trust life – if one of your plans does not happen, if a friend at work seems pre occupied or not attentive to your needs rather than discuss it with them, rather than allow yourself to become enraged or upset, just open up to the day and just see what it brings forward to you.

It may be that not chatting with your normal friend at work means you get to communicate with someone else at work and see another side to them. Do not judge too quickly, do not react too quickly. If your boss yells at you first thing in the morning just open up to it, picture yourself like a flower in the morning sun still with dew on you opening to the sun, open to the experience, the day. Rather than complaining about it all day, just be there and open to the experience, just wait before you get upset and see what else the day will bring. Or you may immediately complain to others, as this is your past behavioural pattern, but after this just calm yourself down enough to just be there and trust that life itself will bring balance back into your day. Just be open, just continue with your work and your day, do not let the ranting's within your mind dominate, allow them to run through your mind like leaves being blown in the wind but do not act upon them, refrain from giving into them, and just wait and see what else the day will bring.

You may soon have another interaction with your boss, and they may seem more subdued apologetic even for their outburst, or you may witness someone putting pressure on them, just wait and trust that life will even things out. There is no need for retort or vengeance, a getting back at them attitude just be alert and trust your day, open as much as you can, be still as much as you can, just let go and sink back into who you are – just drift, rather than row through your day, and take note at the end of it, if it did even out or not. Or if you continue with this you may notice that in a day or two things even out, go back to normal, float along more swiftly. Your boss may even apologise, your boss may do you a favour, if you are alert you may begin to see, how the energy which sustains life – love, is behind everything, and in the end heals and cures and fixes all and everything you need do nothing.

The best thing you can do for you and your family and your life, is simply get out of your own way. Rather than choosing hostile emotion to grapple with the injustices of life, instead open up to them, surrender to them with a heightened awareness that you are not necessarily letting your boss or friend get away with anything, you are instead seeing beyond and behind them to the energy of love, acceptance and life which will continue onwards with your bests interests at heart as you too are part and parcel of it. The greater awareness you have of this very simple fact, the more you voluntarily, look behind the surface of things and trust that all will work out in the end, the better off you will be.

This attitude of let go towards life, of trusting life, of seeing beyond what seems to be – of knowing that in the end your material world will expire and love the essence of the universe will still survive, the more in tune with life you will feel. The less you will get caught up in the temporary knots of the mind, and twist and turn unnaturally into a web of confusion, depression and anxiety. All too often this is what you are doing, you are allowing hidden fears that exist within your mind to provoke you into unnecessary action which injects more energy into your problems making them even more luminous scary and debilitating. Take the energy and the fear out of them, focus instead on trusting life and opening up into each day, each moment, and just see what happens right in front of your eyes.

To help you achieve this, some of you may like to start a **Being Receptive Journal** where you journal your day, highlighting difficulties throughout the day and times or moments where you were able to open up and trust life rather than cower in need and fear and struggle and fight with what was happening and make it all so much worse. OR you could highlight opportunities where you could have been receptive and were not, so that in the following days you may have greater leverage to do so. Noting your failures and successes in this regard will help you to work through the whole idea of being receptive – and of just allowing life to make the first move.

Journaling is not about scolding yourself for not being receptive – it is not about having to do the right thing, follow a set course of action. Journaling is simply a light-hearted personal method that you have of bringing greater awareness of receptivity into your life. It does not matter if you still continued to get caught up in life, to overreact to what other people have said or done, what matters is that your awareness of what is going on, is growing and deepening each and every day. Your awareness of how you interact with life is more important even than being receptive – this is not about me giving you some agenda that you have to fulfil to please me, to gain my affection attention and approval. This is about you gradually incorporating an increasing diorama of skills and tools into your current life coping strategy tool box. So that you can make more informed decisions, so that you can feel more confident with the choices you are making, so that you can see how your choices are impacting and influencing your life, and then feel secure that you have other methods or ways of dealing with problems that may prove more beneficial for you than your current tools.

Learning a new way of interacting while on earth will of course seem strange or even perhaps unnecessary at times, everyone else does not appreciate its value, everyone else is going in the opposite direction, everyone else throws their emotion, judgement and blame onto others, why should you have to be different? Of course my response to this is that 'you want freedom from this enslavement, you have seen how throwing your emotions onto others, how avoiding, ignoring, neglecting, yelling at, or fighting with others makes you feel, and you have seen how it worsens any situation'.

Only by trusting in the goodness of life no matter what appears to be, will you be able to transcend emotion and the murkiness of life. Only by opening so that you can feel the light, the energy, the wholeness offered to you in each and every moment by the Universe will you gradually wipe away the pain, the heartache, the mistrust, the memories, the fear and the delusion that all of you contend with on a daily basis. It does not matter how much you assess or go over your history your past, your childhood experiences, it does not matter how sincere you are to overcome the restraints of earthly life, if you cannot trust, cannot feel, cannot sense the goodness lying behind it all, if you cannot open to allow light to penetrate, you will fail in your attempts.

This is good news as it makes this process very simple and easy, it is so simple children can do it, and they do it naturally. Just by learning to be receptive within each and every moment just by allowing yourself to open to the light and the goodness within you, the bliss inside you, the enormity of love within you, you begin to dissipate all that currently thwarts and compromises you. Thus you do not need a never-ending list of things to do to eradicate or transcend the density of life, you simply open up, receive light and goodness and then bring it back down with you into life, into your family into your relationships, your environments, and this energy itself, although seemingly invisible and transparent has the ability to heal and transform. You need do nothing.

This is why I come to share this wonderful news with you my Beloved Ones, this is why I come forward for you at this time, and this is why also that you have been drawn to this material. Take heed and allow yourself to feel the wonder of this, the grace, the magic, as more real than any gnome, fairy, or wizard does the Universe have the ability to amaze and inspire you. You just need to learn how to watch and to see the ways in which the universe bends and turns, and doubles back on itself just to assist you, enlighten you, comfort you, amuse you, make you laugh, make you see the beauty of which you are part. For when all is said and done the Universe will pervade, love pervades and just is, it is not under attack from some evil force, it is not held hostage to the whims within your mind, no the Universe just is. It is not off in outer space somewhere, it is here with you, within you, it is a part of you and a part of every other living thing – this is all that matters, this is all you need to know – you can adjust or change your life so that you feel it suits you better but at the end of the day it makes no difference to the Universe – for all will simply soak back into the Universal Energy in the end.

Realising this is your freedom – knowing and accepting that in the end none of it matters, the end result will still be the same is crucial to your liberation. While you continue on as you are thinking that each decision you make is life or death, are you bound to be consumed with confusion and dread, in the end it does not matter. You are free to do what you choose, you are to be held captive by no one, there is no heaven and no hell, there is no ignorance or enlightenment, it is all the same, everything soaks back into the universal energy. It does not matter if you marry a rich handsome man or a not so handsome poor one, in the end it will all be the same. It does not matter if you get the promotion at work or not in the end it all works out the same. The little bumps and corners in the road of life disappear into the nothingness from which they came once you pass through them, they can then hold no power over you, so too the ones in your future, they are pale, diluted, impotent, for in the end somehow it all works out the same.

This ensures that you are always where you are meant to be, for in truth there is no where you need be, you are already within the universe, you are already a living, breathing, feeling part of the universe and like a small atom or molecule you simply float along within it. Just because you may be encased in a cell that is not aware of other cells does not matter in the end, all that matters is that you are part of the universe, and the universe is part of you.

So my Beloved Ones fear not – be bold with your decisions and take more liberties than currently you allow yourself to take, and fear no dire consequence or lightning strike – just be open to what is around you, so that you can feel the shimmer of life, so that you can feel the enormity of it, the specialness of it, the harmony, joy and reverence, any small act, small insignificant place or interaction can open you to an outpouring of universal energy if you allow. Touching someone spontaneously who is scared or unwell, looking up at the sky for no good reason while waiting at the traffic lights, stopping and waiting and opening to your husband when he is nattering on about nothing so that you can really hear him, appreciate him, be with him, all these moments and each and every other moment within your life can thrust you instantaneously into the pulsing, vibrating passage of light and life that interacts and swirls within your environment.

The more you allow yourself to open, to just stop, to just be without having to do anything, without having to try and be in moment, by just being receptive, by just sinking back into who you are, by just listening when someone is talking and that's all, you begin to sense with time a very light and gentle current of energy swirling within you, this current makes you feel stronger, more aligned, more connected to where you are and who you are with. These small moments and awareness will grow, will come back in unexpected moments and will eventually lead into a very solid path, a solid connection to this force.

All the while knowing that you are within it already.

Feel and see the power that this awareness could possibly give you, knowing that everyday when you are tired in the morning, yawning and not really wanting to go to work when you are pouring that first cup of coffee when you are staring vacantly out the window, that you can allow this very moment to open you up to the pulsating, dancing energy surrounding you that is you. Watch the trees blow in the gentle breeze or wind, it is like the leaves are dancing, they are enjoying the ride, they are loving this………… so too the birds chirping in the trees, singing to each other courting each other….. They sense and feel the dynamic rhythm of the Universal force. Take notice, and just allow yourself to sink back into yourself as if you are sinking back under the sheets within you. Here lies much comfort, strength, purpose and meaning.

Allow yourself these moments where space exists within your mind, allow this space to pervade your mind, allow this space to open you to mind with no thought, allow the space to descend. Some people may feel tingly on their scalp, or they may sense some vibration around them, on the top of their head, to some it may feel like a heaviness descending, as if a liquid has been injected into the top of the scalp, the mind, others will see light, others will become dizzy, others will just feel or hear an intense buzzing, but there will be this immense sense of openness, spaciousness, clarity and calm within the mind, these elements will always be present.

More and more as you stop even briefly to just close your eyes for a moment or two when you experience this, you will recognise this energy, when it comes. This is not to be feared or made light of, this is a significant occurrence, which although it seems so very natural just like the buzzing of the bees, or the chirping of the birds, the blowing of the breeze, these small instances are highly important and significant, they are reconnecting you to the Universal Energy. The more you surrender to these moments the more they will return, and return and return. They will come when you least expect it, and you should wait with a calm patience and receptivity, not an anguish or impatience to get to the top of the ladder. You must be sincere, and you must appreciate these moments when they come. Let them teach you how to flow with life, how to ride the current of life, do not despair when they disappear, remind yourself that they will return, just give yourself unlimited time and approval to continue with life in the manner that you are – knowing that you are not off course, that you are and always will be amid the stream of Universal Energy, of life….

This perception cancels out duality, rather than continuing with a disassociated or polarised view of the world, suddenly you begin to turn in on yourself towards your centre which is balanced inclusive and whole. This will help you to stay balanced in all your interactions and situations on earth. Currently you swing from one extreme to the other, by becoming sad you invite and entice excitement and happiness into your life, by being happy and excited you invite sadness and meaninglessness in. By being angry you invoke fear and mistrust, by being fearful guilty you invoke anger. Thus just as you accept one emotion into your mind and being another has already left its gate and is headed toward you full speed.

Some people are more even tempered, slower to show these steady stream of emotions, but this is not better this is worse, the emotions still exist, they simply suppress and repress, so that these energies have no choice but to emanate outwards to those surrounding that individual causing greater havoc and crisis within the even tempered person's life. There is no escape from duality, from the never-ending cycle of emotion or energy that manifests and supports the foundations of earthly life. You are compelled almost against your will to experience the opposite just by accepting some small emotion/energy into your field of reference. This is why things always seem so topsy turvy on earth. This is why the things you forget about suddenly come back and hit you in the face, you are creating day by day what emotions, people, circumstances you will live with, just by entertaining their opposite. The more you seek positivity and happiness, the more sadness and despair will creep into your psyche. The more angry and aggressive you become the greater amounts of guilt and shame will you experience. This is all energetic, and the only cure, the only cure, is to return to your centre which is unmoved by any emotion, so that you can at last set yourself free from duality, this up and down emotional rollercoaster ride that all of you are on.

This is where these moments of light and spaciousness come in...... they automatically and naturally bring you back to the middle of the scale, so that you are not weighing down one side so heavily that it is waiting for the slightest move so that it can ping back up again. So that the opposite can come in. These moments of just being, of spaciousness, of no thought or reduced thought within your mind, are like taking a deep breath where no weights are being placed on either side of the scale. This process naturally refreshes and rejuvenates your whole being, your mind, your physiology, your body, this is where true relaxation and effervescence come from.

If you took note you would already realise that the things you seek most in life are pursuits which help your mind to slow down, to stop, and to obliterate thought. Extreme sportsmen, rock climbers, snow boarders, surfers, racing car drivers all speak about how when in the zone, when they are doing what they really love, when their adrenalin is coursing rapidly through their body that they experience a sense of peace, of clarity, of zoning everything else out until there is only them and the car wheel, or them and the rock, them and the board and the wave, this is essentially an orgasm there is no thought, the person accesses a place beyond thought, though still within the mind. Great musicians, dancers, artists, theologians, poets also speak about this. This is where you leave the normal mind behind and access a place where thought does not enter – this is where you meet existence face to face. You may also at the same time be facing a literal death on a rock face, on a wave, but here you are free for the first time from guilt, pain and regret, obligation, planning, life, here you are free just to be. This provides immense joy, immense peace and satisfaction, and is the reason so many chase extreme adventure and pursuits, as once they have tasted this, the desire to taste it again and again is ever-present.

Nothing else can compare to this experience and many a sportsman places himself in very precarious situations to achieve this sense – but this place will also come to you to everyone in and amongst the everyday. All you need do is become more and more aware and in tune with it, the more you take notice of it, the more you will see it, the more it will visit. Thus no need to also seek out your normal addictions, the pokies, shopping, sex, food to slow your mind even just for a millisecond, as you can do it, totally separate and apart from any other force or situation or pre cursor. Doing it this way, my way without addiction or extreme sports or artistic pursuits actually enables the effects of it to remain for longer, and enables you greater ability to access it more regularly also. This actually gives you greater control and power over your ability to access the no mind, and once you can see you do have power over this, you quickly begin to feel more important, worthwhile, significant and less of a victim within your life.

This leads you into a state of greater meaning and purpose whereby you can see how everything that you are doing on earth has meaning as it gradually allows you to step away from the destruction and devastation that earth is popular for and instead move into a greater perception of harnessing the opportunities within your life, within your day to access the no mind, the existential and to feel a vibrant, pulsating part of it. This deep sense of connection and wholeness that the no mind offers is real and valid and just as important as any of your scientific or even personal pursuits and aims. This is how you access health and wellbeing, no need to go to an acupuncturist, a herbalist, a naturopath, doctor, and chiropractor as your inner health surges forward from the effects of the no mind.

This inner health the no mind frees you from the enslavement of duality, it enables sadness to float through you more easily, and happiness also, and it evens out the bumps in your life and mind, and makes life a place of extreme significance and potency. When you can personally adapt your life and your perception so that you are no longer jumping from one side of the scale to the other, when you are learning to be receptive to each and every moment which enables you to access a place of no thought, of pure existence however briefly, you free yourself from the binds, the heartaches, the nausea that has thwarted your life to date.

What could in all honesty be more imperative than this? What else is going to help you clear your life from the turmoil, the debris, the conflict, misunderstanding, fear and hatred? A new house? Afraid not. A new car? Afraid not. A new husband? Afraid not. A holiday? Afraid not. Underneath you know as you have experienced it first hand that nothing else will suffice. What I am speaking about may seem airy fairy to you – it may be like some childhood happily ever after story that bears no relevance to you or the ordinary – but this is because you have not experienced it first hand, or you cannot remember it. I promise that you have experienced it first hand, you just don't remember it, or you were not alert enough to recognise what the experience actually was. But this experience is not airy fairy, it is not some existential nonsense that cannot be correlated to you amidst the greyness and murkiness of earthly life, it is in truth the key to your liberation, and every time you have had a shopping high, a love high, a movie high, a speed or alcoholic high it has been not because of these pre cursors, but in truth has occurred because you have accessed the airy fairyness, the happy ever after land of the no mind.

This is what Buddha, Jesus and Krishna and all of your saints and deities have tried to show you, but you have failed to grasp the true and vibrant essence at the heart of their message, either because their words have been misconstrued or because you have not attempted for long enough to persevere with the right methods to actualise this.

Thus I come forward today to greet you within your own home, in as easy to understand manner as I can, to show you that you do have the power, the opportunity and control to experience the no mind, as you are already experiencing it but for only a millisecond here or there, and to make it an integral, essential part of who you are and a part of your everyday.

This is not an impossibility, this is real, this can happen, and this is not some dreamy myth that I am sharing to entertain or amuse you. Take heart and know that indeed, if you work with what has been provided here, will much be revealed to you. The ball is in your hands, it is and can only be up to you, but please know that indeed much depends upon your decision.

You are in my heart beloveds

I am Mary

What is Love? Messages from Mary on Love and Fulfilment

Maya

REFERENCES:

1. Isaac Newton – By James Gleick : London : Fourth Estate, 2003.

2. Einstein : A Hundred Years of Relativity – Andrew Robinson : Bath : Palazzo, 2010.

3. Martin Luther's Definition of Faith: An excerpt from "An Introduction to St.Paul's Letter to the Romans," Luther's German Bible of 1522 by Martin Luther. Translated by Rev. Robert E. Smith. Sourced from: www.iclnet.org

Maya

What is Love? Messages from Mary on Love and Fulfilment

www.ingramcontent.com/pod-product-compliance
Lightning Source LLC
Chambersburg PA
CBHW070730160426
43192CB00009B/1388